Going for the
GOLD

ROSTER, U.S. OLYMPIC HOCKEY TEAM

Jim Craig, *North Easton, Mass.;* Bill Baker, *Grand Rapids, Minn.;*
Ken Morrow, *Davison, Mich.;* Jack O'Callahan, *Charlestown, Mass.;*
Mike Ramsey, *Minneapolis, Minn.;* Bob Suter, *Madison, Wis.;*
Neal Broten, *Roseau, Minn.;* Dave Christian, *Warroad, Minn.;*
Steve Christoff, *Richfield, Minn.;* Mike Eruzione, *Winthrop, Mass.;*
John Harrington, *Virginia, Minn.;* Mark Johnson, *Madison, Wis.;*
Rob McClanahan, *St. Paul, Minn.;* Mark Pavelich, *Eveleth, Minn.;*
Buzz Schneider, *Babbitt, Minn.;* Dave Silk, *Scituate, Mass.;*
Eric Strobel, *Rochester, Minn.;* Phil Verchota, *Duluth, Minn.;*
Mark Wells, *St. Clair Shores, Minn.*

Going for the
GOLD

How the U.S. Olympic Hockey Team
Won at Lake Placid

Tim Wendel
With a New Introduction by the Author

DOVER PUBLICATIONS, INC.
Mineola, New York

Bibliographical Note

This Dover edition, first published in 2009, is an unabridged republication of the work originally published by Lawrence Hill & Company, Westport, Conn., in 1980 under the title and subtitle *Going for the Gold: How the U.S. Won at Lake Placid.* A new Introduction to the Dover edition, written by the author, has been specially prepared for this edition.

Library of Congress Cataloging-in-Publication Data

Wendel, Tim.
    Going for the gold : how the U.S. Olympic hockey team won at Lake Placid / Tim Wendel ; with a new introduction by the author. — Dover ed.
        p. cm.
    Originally published: Westport, Conn. : L. Hill, c1980.
    ISBN-13: 978-0-486-47461-8
    ISBN-10: 0-486-47461-5
    1. Hockey—United States. 2. Olympic Winter Games (13th : 1980 : Lake Placid, N.Y.) I. Title.

GV848.4.U6W46 2009
796.9620973—dc22

2009029306

Manufactured in the United States by Courier Corporation
47461501
www.doverpublications.com

Contents

INTRODUCTION TO THE DOVER EDITION   vii

FOREWORD   xi

PART I – HOW THEY WON   1

Chapter 1 – On the Road   3
Chapter 2 – Going for the Gold   26

PART II – MEET THE CHAMPIONS   49

Chapter 3 – The Minnesota Way   51
Chapter 4 – Fleet, Fast and Unlucky   58
Chapter 5 – The Iron Ranger   66
Chapter 6 – The Conehead Who Wouldn't Quit   74
Chapter 7 – The Kid from Bunker Hill   81
Chapter 8 – Shelter from the Storm   90
Chapter 9 – The Midas Touch   102
Chapter 10 – The Best of Both Worlds   112
Chapter 11 – A Modern Myth   123

PART III – STATISTICAL REVIEW   125

ACKNOWLEDGMENTS   132

For Jacqueline, Sarah and Chris

Introduction to the Dover Edition

Hockey was my first love. Even though I went on to write several novels and cover everything from rock and roll to America's Cup sailing, there was always something about the game on ice.

I grew up less than an hour from the Canadian border. Despite such proximity, I didn't really start to skate until I was ten years old. Way too late to excel at such a complicated game, but knowledgeable enough to know the sublime when I stumbled across it.

When I was a boy, my father would sometimes pull the family station wagon over near the escarpment, the dominant land formation in our part of the world. Only a few miles to the west, that jagged silhouette forms the precipice that becomes Niagara Falls. From atop the escarpment, Dad would tune in the CBC from Toronto, a radio signal that dissolved to static down in the valley, closer to home. Together we listened to the Maple Leafs, back when they won Stanley Cup championships.

Thus began my appreciation for hockey. An infatuation that was fostered by playing the game, albeit poorly, and, later on, by my father having season tickets to our new hometown team, the Buffalo Sabres.

Like I said, I loved the sport. Yet it was certainly an acquired taste, barely appreciated in other parts of the country, where I lived years later. The connection and fan base was so regional that one could draw a big ring around the Great Lakes and call it Hockey Land. That's how hard core and out of bounds hockey seemed to be to the U.S. national audience. And that's how the sports world remained until it was turned upside down in 1980.

Back then, fresh out of college, I hadn't planned on covering the Olympic team. I was writing for *Hockey* magazine and trying to catch on with the better-paying glossy magazines in New York. I had a college friend I could bunk with, so I was assigned to cover the NCAA hockey championships in 1979. The Minnesota Golden Gophers and Coach Herb Brooks won the title that spring. When Brooks and seven guys from that team returned to head up the U.S. Olympic squad, I stayed on the story. After all, when the team assembled at JFK International Airport, bound for a training trip to

Scandinavia, I was living close enough so I could drive over and park at the airport for a few bucks. What I'm trying to explain is that the sports world was certainly a simpler, arguably a more innocent place back then. The new kid, a.k.a. me, wanted to write hockey, so why not let him cover these guys who didn't stand a chance against the best in the world? At least that's what my bosses thankfully thought.

Of course, that changed with the last-second tie with Sweden and then the upset victory over Czechoslovakia. Chants of "USA, USA" echoed from the now-packed Olympic Center in Lake Placid. And after defeating the Soviet Union, securing the gold medal by defeating Finland, members of the U.S. Olympic hockey team were household names. For my money, they are still the architects of the biggest series of upsets in sports history.

But when I look back upon those days, I don't immediately flash back to Bill Baker's improbable goal against the Swedes or Mike Eruzione's winner for the ages against the Soviets, or even how a young team found the resolve to come back against the Finns. That's all become highlight reel stuff, forever rolled out when somebody wants to wax on about impossible dreams, miracles and alike.

No, what I remember about those days was being on board before the gold rush. When sometimes I was the only one covering this team. Back when you could get to know the players, even talk strategy with the coaches. Moments that are next to impossible to recreate in today's 24/7 news churn and Internet blogsphere.

After the gold medal ceremony in Lake Placid, the U.S. was eager to embrace its new sports heroes. But, in many ways, it was already too late. The ability to shock the world was forged during those long road trips in the months leading up to Lake Placid. Even though the guys on this team were astounded by the public reaction after the gold medal ceremony, they realized that it had only happened because they had first come together as a team. How fortunate they had been to operate under the radar in the year before the Winter Games. In essence, those times became my password when I began to write *Going for the Gold*.

This was my first book, and it wouldn't have happened without the support and encouragement of many of the guys who took our breath away and made us cheer unabashedly for the red, white and blue. There was the time John Harrington and Eric Strobel diagrammed team breakout plays, so I really understood them. When

I visited Buzz Schneider in northern Minnesota, hard by the Canadian border, he insisted on driving me to the outskirts of town to see the northern lights, in large part because I had come all that way to see his community rink, and to meet his family and friends. In the weeks after Lake Placid, I called Coach Brooks at home. He was overwhelmed with requests by then, and nearly put me off until I said, "JFK Airport. Remember?" We went on to talk for an hour, most of it being about the days leading up to the gold medal. The times when it was just a coach and a bunch of college kids eager to take on the world.

Sometimes a guy gets real, real lucky. Through no plan or scheme of his own, he stumbles upon one of the biggest stories ever. That's the way it was for me, back in 1979–1980. I'm a better writer now, but if anything, I'm still searching for a story as good as this one.

July 2009   TIM WENDEL
Vienna, Virginia

Foreword

I watched my first hockey game when I was eight. I sat down in the living room next to my father and peered at a telecast of "Hockey Night In Canada." The show was, and still is, broadcast Wednesday and Saturday nights from Toronto, Ontario, which is 40 miles northwest of my parents' upstate New York home. After watching that game, I found baseball was still fun, and basketball OK, but nothing surpassed the speed and excitement of hockey.

The sport fascinated and puzzled me. The players seemed to race around the rink with no apparent destination in mind. But as I studied the sport and learned the intricacies of forechecking, passing plays and stickhandling, my heroes became hockey players like Dave Keon, Bobby Orr and Mike Walton. I remember a Christmas vacation when I was 13 or 14 and my family dragged me to a ballet performance of Tchaikovsky's Nutcracker Suite in Toronto. I wanted to stay home and watch the Maple Leafs play the Philadelphia Flyers on television. One of my favorites, Toronto left wing Mike Walton, had scored in the last three games and I wanted to see if he could keep the streak going. During the ballet's intermission I pestered several ushers about the game and whether they knew if Walton had scored. They only laughed, saying they rarely watched hockey.

As soon as the family station wagon rolled into the driveway later that night, I was in front of the television, trying to find out the score. An hour later, my cheers woke up my brothers and sisters when I found out the Leafs and Philadelphia had tied 1-1, and that Walton had scored the lone Toronto goal.

At the age of 15, I tried playing hockey on the organized level, but couldn't keep up with many of my teammates. Most of them had been skating since they were small children. My failure on the ice only brought a deeper appreciation of what I watched on television. Bobby Orr and Dave Keon made their sport into art, and their moves became more extraordinary after I tried to duplicate them.

Even though he was a defenseman, Orr was the premier offensive player of his time. Coming down the ice, he could veer suddenly in any direction and turn in a complete circle. No player could keep up with him, and his twists and spins could have been a part of any figure skating program. Photographs of Orr in action occasionally showed him leaning so far to one side on his skates that the laws of gravity, for that brief moment, seemed not to exist.

Keon was a center with Toronto for many years, and he made a name for himself by defensing players like Orr. Always in motion, back and forth, from one side of the rink to the other, he chased his foes and pestered them into mistakes. A smart player and an exceptional skater, Keon studied his opponents' habits and styles and was often in the right place at the right time to break up a potential scoring rush.

In the Seventies, however, Orr, Keon and players like them took a back seat to many of the problems which beset North American hockey. Since 1967, the National Hockey League had been adding more teams and yesterday's minor leaguers became supposed major league stars. A rival league (the World Hockey Association) formed, salaries rose, and skilled players and respected referees became more difficult to find. The game further deteriorated when the NHL team owners decided to sell the sport to an American television audience. By their decree, a bench-clearing brawl was more entertaining than a goal. League highlight films shown on television, commercials and even in the U.S. Hockey Hall of Fame, featured numerous fights. These antics soon dumped the game into the same category as roller derby and professional wrestling. It became embarrassing to call yourself a hockey fan.

My enthusiasm for hockey was renewed in the summer of 1979 when, as a young sports writer, I first interviewed members of the United States Olympic hockey team. The players came from different parts of the country. Many were from Minnesota and Wisconsin, while others grew up in neighborhoods near Boston and Detroit. The club was given no chance of winning the gold medal at Lake Placid, and the experts predicted that the U.S. would be lucky to finish higher than seventh place. However, there was a mood of fun and a willingness to work hard throughout the team, and I found coach Herb Brooks' plan to field a skating team encouraging. His major priority was speed. The coach wanted fast, intelligent players in the mold of Orr and Keon, and not thugs who were just out to highstick and fight with their opponents. At Lake Placid, the U.S. team's most formidable competitors would be the Soviet Union, a squad of seasoned veterans who often defeated the best the NHL could offer. Besides being brilliant skaters, the Russians are just as effective with their elbows and sticks as any team. Filling a rink full of American "enforcers" would not intimidate the Soviets into defeat. The only way to beat them was to adopt some of their techniques.

And coach Brooks did. He instructed his college stars in the fluid style of skating, passing and constant motion that the Soviets and other European teams practiced. He combined this pattern of play with aggressive forechecking, similar to the way most North American teams played. During the U.S. practices that I attended, the team was taught to perform as a set of interchangeable parts—each player willing to take over on offense and able to help out on defense. Brooks took the shackles off his players. When the Americans had the puck they were encouraged to be creative and innovative; "Your play is an expression of yourself within a framework of friends," Brooks told them.

The U.S. work-outs were unlike anything I had ever seen in youth hockey. The first segment, at least 15 minutes, consisted of stretching and warm-up excercises. The drills that followed emphasized keeping possession of the puck and not dumping it into the opponents' end as most pro teams are prone to do. Off the ice the players lifted weights, played soccer and absorbed more of coach Brooks' slogans. "The whole theme of this team is we can't beat ourselves," Brooks told me. "We have to recognize that we all have different chemistries, we have different personalities, we have different goals and aspirations, we all come from different backgrounds. We just have to melt into a real, tenacious, solidified unit."

Another major reason for the U.S. team's success was the grueling six month schedule of exhibition games that prepared them for Lake Placid. The first month of the 61-game schedule included contests in Holland, Finland and Norway. I was the only member of the press at New York's JFK Airport on September 1 to see the team off to Europe on the first leg of its exhibition schedule. The players were anxious to talk about how much they enjoyed playing "American" hockey.

Bill Baker was so excited about making the club he has postponed his entrance into dental school. Eric Strobel commented that the larger ice surfaces in Olympic hockey would favor this team. Mike Ramsey, only a high school senior two seasons before, said that he would really be "psyched up" playing for his country. I had first met Baker, Strobel, Ramsey and other members of the University of Minnesota Gophers, among them Coach Brooks, at the National Collegiate Athletic Association hockey championship, March 1979, in Detroit. The U.S. team's confidence at JFK was so infectious that after several interviews, I was ready to find my skates and ride off with them to score goals for my country. But then I remembered that I was never much good anyway and decided to pick up pen and paper and write about them instead.

In the months leading up to Lake Placid, I wrote a half-dozen stories on the team and got to know many more of the players. During the 61-game exhibition schedule I kept in touch with them over the phone and interviewed their parents and NHL opponents. I also talked with major spokesmen on college hockey in this country, like Charlie Holt of New Hampshire; Jack Parker of Boston University; Bill Cleary of Harvard; and John Mariucci, former Gophers' coach and now assistant general manager of the Minnesota North Stars.

The week before Christmas I traveled up to Lake Placid for the Pre-Olympic Hockey Tournament. It was good to see friends like Strobel again, and we talked about the team's development, funny incidents that had occurred on the road and the upcoming Olympic Games. For a time I felt like a member of the team. When one of the television networks did a feature on Jim Craig, we stood outside the goalie's hotel door, yelling kiddingly "We want Jimmy. We want Jimmy." The night the U.S. won the game against a Russian team to take first place in the tournament with an undefeated record, the Americans had a midnight curfew. But no one made it—even coach Brooks was at a party miles away. Back at the hotel, his assistant coach, Craig Patrick, was being chased up and down the hallway by a pack of hockey groupies. Out walking around with nothing but a towel around his waist, Patrick had been locked out of his room by some U.S. team member. Strobel and I alerted the groupies in the lobby about Patrick's predicament, and the fun began.

Although the U.S. hockey team sometimes resembled an "Our Gang" comedy, the club was also earnest and talented. The profiles in "Going for the Gold" concentrate on the best examples of these traits: Jack O'Callahan's enthusiasm, Buzz Schneider's experience, captain Mike Eruzione's leadership and Eric Strobel's skating skill. These abilities were the building blocks of the Olympic victories.

For many Americans, the U.S. win at Lake Placid was not only entertaining but it reasserted the qualities we had forgotten as a nation.

"Going for the Gold" is more than an instant replay of what happened at Lake Placid. This book tells of my visits to many of the players' hometowns and my talks with their parents, coaches and friends. It attempts to recapture and describe the spirit that made them winners at Lake Placid.

PHOTO BY PETE HALPERN

Across the country, those who love and play hockey are happy. Their joy is because of 20 young men who for two weeks made the sport as exciting and as beautiful as it has ever been. The 1980 U.S. Olympic hockey team will be remembered as the club that gave hockey and a nation another chance to call ourselves winners.

PART I

How They Won

PHOTO BY PETE HALPERN

Bill Baker and Dave Christian celebrate Mike Eruzione's winning goal against the Russians.

CHAPTER 1

On the Road

The use of traveling is to regulate imagination
by reality, and instead of thinking how things may
be, to see them as they are.

—Samuel Johnson

The traffic jam began a couple of miles outside of Manhattan and continued bumper to bumper east toward John F. Kennedy International Airport. It was the first day of September, and under a blazing sun the temperature and humidity hovered near 90 degrees. Along the highway, several cars had pulled off to the side, their radiators boiling over and their owners standing dumbfounded and helpless next to the seething crates.

Those whose machines still ran, sped by, their air conditioners pushed to the max and their FM radios turned up loud. Over the airwaves, Blondie sang how love was just "a pain in the ass," and Neil Young lamented that "in the field of opportunity it's plowing time again."

At the Scandinavian Airlines, JFK terminal, departure time for the evening plane to Oslo, Norway, was hours away. There were no other flights that afternoon and the ticket takers had little to do except talk and laugh among themselves and watch the cars pass by. The terminal was air-conditioned, and frequently people walking outdoors in the heat would step through the sliding glass doors and into the building to cool off. The visitors would walk around, looking at the color photographs of white glaciers and blue fiords, until an airline employee approached and asked if he could help. Politely replying, "No, we're just looking," the intruders would retreat back outside. The employees then returned to their afternoon conversations.

The terminal was quiet until 3:32 P.M., when loud screeches were heard outside. As heads turned, the doors to three vans opened, and some 25 young men jumped out and began digging through the mound of brown leather baggage in the vehicles' storage bins; each trying to find his particular piece of luggage. The group tumbled toward the terminal doors, swapping suitcases and hanging bags along the way and once inside, they dumped the gear on the floor and doubled back to the vans for more. Within minutes, the lobby was a heap of bags, hockey sticks and equipment. When the airline officials tried to transfer the luggage out to the plane bound for

Oslo, the conveyor belt broke. The exasperated ticket takers sighed and shook their heads. Meanwhile, their visitors had taken over. Yelling instructions to each other, they clambered over the ticket counter and started passing the gear out to the loading area in the manner of a Chinese fire drill. " Just trying to help out," one participant said.

It looked like a scene from a Keystone Kops movie. Actually, it was the U.S. Olympic hockey team on their way to Norway.

The American squad that took off from JFK on that hot September afternoon was at the beginning of a long journey that would take them on a three-week tour of Europe, and then a four-month road trip through North America, until they reached their final destination—the Olympic Games in Lake Placid, New York.

The Olympians were a collection of inexperienced college stars and unknown minor leaguers. Most of the collegiate players were used to playing only 25 to 30 games a year, and those who tried out for NHL teams were bounced from one farm club to another, unable to find a pro team willing to sign them. The voyage of six months and 61 games would transform this unpolished band of luggage lackeys into a close-knit team capable of defeating the more mature squads from Russia, Finland and Czechoslovakia.

Visions of adventure and foreign lands danced in the players' heads as they started for Europe. However, in any journey, there is an ordeal, a task which must be completed before any player can reach the heights of achievement. The test each American athlete faced was being named to the Olympic roster. Twenty-six players were on the U.S. traveling club, but only 20 would be in the line-up at Lake Placid. The European trip soon became the first trial of the players' patience and determination to make the team. They traveled long distances, often at night by bus or train to games. There was little time for sightseeing and when the team did have a couple of free hours, they were usually miles away from any city lights.

"The Europe trip was a lot of traveling and carrying our own bags," says player Dave Christian. "Before we went over, all we heard was how lucky we were, how we were going to see Europe. That got to be a big joke on the team—aren't we so lucky? About all we saw was the inside of hockey rinks and the inside of hotels. We'd play a game, get on a bus or a train, end up somewhere else and play another game."

The person with the final say over which players would make the Olympic team was U.S. coach Herb Brooks. He made it clear during the European trip that he wanted hard workers on his club. Before a game with Norway, Brooks warned his team that they were not hustling and that their play was lackluster and shabby. His warning went unheeded, and Norway tied the U.S., 3-3. After the game, Brooks called his team out of the locker room and directed them in an exhausting practice in front of 10,000 puzzled Norwegians. After 45 minutes, the U.S. team doctor, V. George Nagobads, yelled at Brooks, "Herbie, Herbie, stop, stop, they've had enough." The weary team learned its lesson and, the following evening, trounced Norway, 9-0.

One of coach Brooks' many sayings was "I'd cut my own brother to make a better hockey team." With many coaches that is an empty threat, but Brooks meant what he said. From the time of the team's selection, Brooks knew his players would dislike, perhaps even hate him. However, with six athletes to drop from the team, Brooks choose to be aloof and separate from his team in order to remain objective. "If we had been able to get down to 20 guys on the first day, things could have been different," he says. "I had to let the players know that I respected everybody. I didn't want to get close to a couple if I couldn't get close to them all. I wanted to do everything I could to be called an honest S.O.B."

The former Minnesota coach was determined to treat all his players equally, even if it meant ignoring close friends like former Minnesota players Buzz Schneider and Les Auge. "He wasn't the guy I used to have beers with at Stub and Herb's (a campus hangout near the University of Minnesota campus)," says Schneider. "I knew why he did it, but it was tough. But I wasn't going to let him cut me. I was going to work as hard as I could to make that team."

"I know one thing, that for guys like me he made it a lot tougher," says Eric Strobel, also a former Minnesota player. "He never really talked to the guys from Minnesota on this team. I guess he figured he couldn't play favorites."

Brooks criticized all his players, constantly pointing out their mistakes and rarely praising them. His insults were legendary. Once in practice, he told Strobel that his brain was just "a five-pound fart in between his ears." By design or chance, Brooks got his players' undivided attention, and by playing the villain, he brought his team together. Players that once knew each other only as rivals, became united under Brooks' rule.

"When he screwed one of us, all of us got pissed off," Jack O'Callahan says. "We'd sit there and say, 'We'll get him, we'll get that Herbie.' Looking back on it that's probably exactly what he wanted us to do."

Other players, like John Harrington, contend that many of Brooks' moves were more fortunate than brilliant. "People ask Herb if he did something for a psychological reason and he'll never say. He'll just sit there with that smug look on his face.

"The one thing about that guy which makes him unique is that he is so puzzling to everybody." Harrington continues. "You can hate him, but you're never sure if he's on the level with all this stuff he's pulling or if he's just a goofy guy and doesn't know what he's doing. Like some of the things he did—the constant line switching, the way he ran his practices—didn't make sense, but then all of a sudden things would work out and he's got that look on his face again."

At the age of 22, Herb Brooks was one of the last players to be dropped from the 1960 U.S. Olympic team. He, Robert Dupuis and Larry Alm were cut from the squad to make room for Bill Cleary, his brother Bob and John Mayasich only two weeks before the team left for Squaw Valley, California, the site of the 1960 Olympiad. Ironically, Bill Cleary, now coach at Harvard, became one of Brooks' close friends and a member of his Olympic advisory staff.

After the Americans upset Russia, Canada and Czechoslovakia to win the 1960 gold medal, Brooks collared U.S. coach Jack Riley and told him "Well, you must have made the right decision. You won." Twenty years later, the statement still sums up the logical, unemotional and always pragmatic coach of the 1980 U.S. team.

Born in St. Paul, Minnesota, Brooks was the oldest of three children. An outstanding high school hockey player, Brooks later was on the University of Minnesota team. He graduated in 1962 with a degree in psychology, and used what he learned in the classroom in motivating his players. Brooks played on the 1964 and 1968 U.S. Olympic teams, and was a five-time member of the U.S. national team. He had planned to go into the insurance business before accepting a coaching position at the University of Minnesota, where he led the Gophers to national championships in 1974, 1976 and 1979.

The 1980 Olympic team was Brooks' great challenge. He had only 10 months to forge a team that could be competitive with the world's best. The first problem the Olympic coach faced was persuading the top U.S. amateurs even to try out. Usually, America's best players pass up the Olympics and sign with a professional team as soon as their college eligibility runs out. While the rest of the world sets its sights on the gold medal, North American players aim for the Stanley Cup and the big money of professional hockey. However, Brooks presented a new plan which many potential Olympians saw as a stepping stone to the NHL and not as a detriment to their

UNIVERSITY OF MINNESOTA PHOTO

Herb Brooks, former coach at the University of Minnesota and U.S. Olympic coach.

careers. The U.S. coach put together a rugged exhibition schedule against pro and international opponents, better competition than minor league teams have. Another inducement was that each player chosen to the Olympic traveling team received a salary of at least $7,200 for six months plus expenses. Again, it was better than, or on par with, minor league clubs.

"I had to convince everybody on the Olympic committee that we had to be innovative and creative this year to keep these people available. If you don't have the talent, nothing is going to fall into shape." Brooks says. "I wanted to persuade the NHL teams that drafted many of these players that the Olympic team could develop them better than they could if the players turned pro right away. For the players, I offered a proposal where they could have their cake and eat it too. They could play in the Olympics and then turn pro almost immediately."

Finally, Brooks made it clear that he was going to take the time to rate every player who tried out. An advisory committee of professional and college coaches was formed. "I didn't want an 'I, me, myself' organization." Brooks says. "There's a wealth of hockey talent in terms of expertise around the country, so I wanted to get those people involved."

Brooks brought in coaches like Wisconsin's Bob Johnson, Harvard's Bill Cleary, New Hampshire's Charlie Holt, Colorado College's Jeff Sauer and Boston University's Jack Parker. Some were former rivals. In 1976, Parker and Brooks clashed at the NCAA college championships. After Brooks' Minnesota team defeated BU in a semi-final game, Parker accused the Gopher coach of playing "goon" hockey. Brooks replied that if he had the time and the money he would have sued. Four years later, Parker was on Brooks' advisory committee because he wanted the best possible team selected.

Brooks' "We, Us and Ourselves" approach worked and more than 400 players came out for the Olympic team. Armed with charts and checklists that graded everything from how a player skated backwards to his mental attitude, Brooks and his committee set out to rate all the prospects. There were regional try-out camps across the country with the best players selected to appear at the National Sports Festival in July 1979 at Colorado Springs. Some, like Wisconsin's Mark Johnson and BU's Jim Craig, were named to the Olympic team without appearing at Colorado Springs. They were injured or sick, and Brooks and his committee had seem them play enough anyway. But others, like University of Minnesota at Duluth's John Harrington and Wisconsin's Bob Suter won berths on the team with their inspired play at the festival. There were 68 players at the Colorado Springs Festival and Brooks' committee judged them daily by rotating assignments. For instance, Harvard's Cleary would watch the defensemen for one session and centers the next. Meanwhile, Wisconsin's Johnson or Colorado College's Sauer would take over, observing the defensemen.

When the try-outs ended, Brooks huddled with his advisors, and then announced that the following players had made his team:

Player	Age	Previous Team	Hometown
Goaltenders			
Jim Craig	22	Boston University	North Easton, Mass.
Bruce Horsch	23	Nova Scotia (AHL)	Hastings, Minn.
Steve Janaszak	22	Univ. of Minnesota	White Bear Lake, Minn.
Defensemen			
Les Auge	26	Oklahoma City (CHL)	St. Paul, Minn.
Bill Baker	22	Univ. of Minnesota	Grand Rapids, Minn.
Jack Hughes	21	Harvard	Somerville, Mass.
Ken Morrow	22	Bowling Green	Davison, Mich.
Jack O'Callahan	21	Boston University	Charlestown, Mass.
Mike Ramsey	18	Univ. Of Minnesota	Minneapolis, Minn.
Gary Ross	25	Klagenfurt (Austria)	Roseau, Minn.
Bob Suter	22	Univ. of Wisconsin	Madison, Wis.
Forwards			
Neal Broten	19	Univ. of Minnesota	Roseau, Minn.
Dave Christian	20	North Dakota U.	Warroad, Minn.
Steve Christoff	21	Univ. of Minnesota	Richfield, Minn.
Ralph Cox	22	Univ. of New Hampshire	Braintree, Mass.
Dave Delich	22	Colorado College	Eveleth, Minn.
Mike Eruzione	24	Toledo (IHL)	Winthrop, Mass.
John Harrington	22	Univ. of Minnesota-Duluth	Virginia, Minn.
Mark Johnson	21	Univ. of Wisconsin	Madison, Wis.
Rob McClanahan	21	Univ. of Minnesota	St. Paul, Minn.
Mark Pavelich	21	Univ. of Minnesota-Duluth	Eveleth, Minn.
Buzz Schneider	24	Milwaukee (IHL)	Babbitt, Minn.
Dave Silk	21	Boston University	Scituate, Mass.
Eric Strobel	21	Univ. of Minnesota	Rochester, Minn.
Phil Verchota	22	Univ. of Minnesota	Duluth, Minn.
Mark Wells	21	Bowling Green	St. Clair Shores, Mich.

Brooks should be given a lot of credit for the team that was selected," BU's Parker says. "In the past, it was usually Western or WCHA (Western Collegiate Hockey Association) players who were picked. But from the point of view of the Eastern people he was extremely fair. I don't think anyone could have done a better, more rational job."

The U.S. team was young. But even with an average of less than 22 years, it remained one of the best assemblages of talent for any U.S. amateur team. Among the high draft picks who decided to stay out of pro hockey for six months was Mike Ramsey, a 19-year-old

Dave Christian scored his first professional goal within seconds of entering his first NHL game. Here, he waits for a teammate's pass while Dave Keon, former star with the Toronto Maple Leafs and now with the Hartford Whalers, moves in to stop the play.

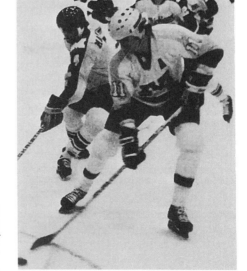

Steve Christoff prepares to shovel the puck into the Michigan net during a WCHA game. Christoff set a playoff scoring record for rookies after joining the NHL.

defenseman from Minneapolis. The No. 1 pick of the Buffalo Sabres in the 1979 amateur draft, Ramsey was the first American player ever selected in the NHL's first round. Other prospective NHL stars included Steve Christoff, the No. 2 choice of the Minnesota North Stars; Bill Baker, picked in the third round of the 1978 draft by Montreal; and Rob McClanahan, the Sabres' No. 3 selection in 1978. The player with the most impressive Olympic legacy was Dave Christian, the No. 2 choice of the Winnipeg Jets in the 1979 draft. His father, Bill Christian, now a hockey-stick manufacturer in Warroad, Minnesota, scored the winning goal in the 3-2 victory over the Soviets in the 1960 Olympics. Dave also has two uncles who have played hockey in the Olympics.

Despite such stars, a great deal of work had to be done before the Americans dared dream about winning a medal, let alone the gold. Brooks had only a few months to teach his team a new style of play.

Most teams in North America play "dump-and-run," where a player shoots the puck into his opponents' defensive zone and then chases after it. If he is persistent and lucky he might regain the puck in a scoring position. The game, however, usually becomes boring when the two teams with capable stickhandlers and passers face-off, both playing this style. Instead of exciting end-to-end rushes and offensive plays that require speed and deception, the game becomes repetitive and predictable. The Europeans, especially the Soviets, found that the traditional concept of dumping the puck in and of staying in the lanes (right wing on right side, center in the middle and left wing on the left side) to be outdated. International hockey is played on rinks 100 feet wide, compared with 85 feet wide ice surfaces in the NHL. This means more open ice and a greater emphasis on mobile players and creative offenses.

Brooks' new system of hockey—dubbed "American hockey"— combined the aggressive forechecking prowess of North American hockey with the open-ice tactics of the Europeans. The key to the U.S. coach's plan was control of the puck. He constantly told his team that if they hung onto the puck they would, more often than not, win the game. "In other words, I don't want to punt on first down," he told his team. "It's stupid. You work like hell to get the puck and then to give it up and force other teams into mistakes—it's the law of diminishing returns. You will have to give the puck up at times, there's no question. But I don't want to give it up as a first priority.

"In football they all don't run the same offense or play the same defense. I just think that hockey should be looked at differently than it has been in the past. Some things should be questioned, rather than a coach picking whatever system he wants to play. There's a lot of good systems, but I don't think we should all be playing the same one."

At times, especially during the first two and half months the team was together, the players found American hockey frustrating to learn. The club did win seven of 10 games in Europe. However, they often intimidated their foes with resounding body-checks and high sticks. When they returned to North America in late September, they got a rude awakening, losing four straight games to NHL opponents. The U.S. dropped the first contest, 4-2, to the Minnesota North Stars before a crowd of 13,084 at the MET Center in Bloomington. "They came to see the old Gophers," remembers Minnesota coach Glen Sonmor. "We got some shock. They booed us." The next night, in Des Moines, the Americans were soundly thrashed, 9-1, by the St. Louis Blues. Four nights later, the U.S. team was again humiliated as they were defeated, 6-1, by the Atlanta Flames. The Washington Capitals were the last NHL team to beat the Americans, but they did it with a late goal to win narrowly, 5-4. "We did lose that one," says Rob McClanahan, "but at least we did better than the other ones. We should have won that game."

Brooks kept pushing his players, teaching them his new style. He often repeated colorful sayings in practice and in the locker room to get his philosophy across. While talking with his team, he would rummage through his pockets, pulling out wrinkled pieces of yellow paper with slogans scribbled on them. The catchwords were reiterated so often that several players—John Harrington, Dave Silk, and Mike Eruzione—put together a notebook of Brooks' mottos, entitled "The Best of Brooksisms." Among the U.S. coach's best were:

"Don't dump the puck in. That went out with short pants."

"You're playing worse every day, and right now you're playing in the middle of next month."

"There's confusion in our design, but there's method in our madness."

"Passes come from the heart and not from the stick."

"You can't be common because the common man goes nowhere. You've got to be uncommon."

"Gentlemen, you don't have enough talent to win on talent alone."

Even though his team often laughed and cursed at him behind his back, when Brooks posted the new line combinations or announced who would sit out the upcoming games, the locker room fell silent. But as soon as he left, the place again became noisy, full of laughter, and as one player said, "Like a study hall with the teacher out of the room."

UNIVERSITY OF MINNESOTA PHOTO

Neal Broten is stopped by the Notre Dame goalkeeper. After the Olympics, Broten wanted to return to collegiate hockey.

Neal Broten and Dave Christian, who grew up 20 miles away from each other in northwestern Minnesota, were the U.S. resident clowns. The duo were infamous for putting ice cubes in other players' boots, talcum powder in gloves and covering shin pads and jockstraps in a thick layer of tape. A clever playmaker, Broten was called the "best freshman ever to have played at the University of Minnesota" by none other than coach Brooks. In the locker room, Broten was teased for his voice, which would break into a Mickey Mouse-like pitch when he got excited. "Neal had no business being 19 years old," says Olympic teammate John Harrington, "because he acted more like he was 12."

Meanwhile, Broten's buddy, Christian, seemed much older than his 20 years. As Broten jabbered away, rarely about anything significant, a grinning Christian sat next to him ready to deliver a funny one-liner. Before one game, as the team suited up in the locker room, Broten broke into a pep talk. "Let's go guys, we got to do it. Got to get going, got to want it," he said, his voice breaking. "I don't want to have to go out there and score three goals all by myself to win this thing."

Rob McClanahan drops the puck back to a teammate as the U.S. play possession hockey.

"You won't have to," Christian said, "I'll put one in for you."

Rob McClanahan, one of the most intense competitors on the team, bore the brunt of many of Broten and Christian's tricks. Before a game or practice, McClanahan often sat in his stall, painstakingly inspecting his sticks—checking the curve of the blade and the tape job—making sure each was the same, "Robby took things a little too seriously." Christian recalls. "Sometimes walking out on the ice I'd accidently run into his sticks, knock them over, you know?"

As the season progressed, the team began giving McClanahan standing ovations when he got on the team bus or applauding when he came out on the ice for practice. When he tried saying something in the locker room, the team shouted him down with chants of "Robby, Robby." A flustered McClanahan often said, "Jesus, it's better for me not to say anything at all."

"The guys got on my back a lot, but it was all in jest," McClanahan remembers. "I don't know why me. I guess they liked me or something—that's what they keep telling me. I used to be a prankster at Minnesota a couple years ago, but I kept getting the worst of it, so I decided to change my ways, but those guys just kept on needling me. At times I'd had some trouble taking it, and I'd had enough. And other times I smiled and didn't let it bother me."

Another team clown was Dave Silk. A native of Scituate, Massachusetts, he was forever talking about living in New England. "They're some guys on this team that grew up in Boston." he told

Dave Silk, playing for the Boston University Terriers, maintains his position in front of the opponents' goal.

his Minnesota teammates, "the rest of you all wish you did." Such talk continued until Phil Verchota, a former Gopher from Duluth growled, "Watch it, Silky. You know what Herbie said—'Don't get regional.'" The phrase soon became a standing team joke, and whenever someone started boasting about his hometown, a teammate would say, "Don't get regional."

There was usually an on-going dialogue between Verchota and Eruzione. The two prepared for games by calling each other names. "If I had ever come into the locker room and Phil had asked how I was doing today, I probably wouldn't have known what to do." Eruzione admits. "He was always on my case.

Dave Silk in Beanpot game against Harvard in 1977.

"It was a fun, relaxed kind of locker room," he adds. "And I don't think Herb was the whole reason why we were so close. Herb was fortunate to have the kind of players he had. Sure, he selected us and brought us together. I can't take anything away from Herbie, he did an incredible job. But I want to give us as much credit as possible too. We continued what he started. We could have just as easily said, 'Forget this.' "

Although a lively uninhibited place, the U.S. locker room could also be quiet for those players like Eric Strobel and John Harrington who liked to collect their thoughts before a game.

"There was a lot of fun, but really there weren't many screamers or rah-rahs," Strobel says. "Everyone just let everyone else prepare in his own way. I know when I was on the football team in high school, everybody would have to be yelling or something like that (in the locker room) and I'd find someplace to hide, sit back and try to relax a little. On this team I could do that."

Harrington spent his time in the locker room, slowly putting on his equipment and thinking about what he had to do in certain game situations or, as he said, "taking the game apart in my mind." Even Strobel and Harrington, though, got involved in some revelry. At Strobel's urging, Harrington would launch into his battle cry, which sounded like infield chatter in baseball. "C'mon, c'mon, here we go, red, white, white, red," he would shout.

Sometimes, the team's exuberance went too far. In mid-December, after its four consecutive losses to NHL opponents, the U.S. team had its first contest against the Canadian Olympic team. The Americans won the first game, 7-2, in Hibbing, Minnesota. The team arrived back in the Twin Cities late that evening and Jack Hughes, Dave Silk and several other players borrowed assistant coach Craig Patrick's car to drive back to the Burnsville apartment complex where most of the team lived. Burnsville is about 15 minutes south of the Twin Cities, and on the way back to the apartments, the Patrick station wagon was nearly run off the road by an intoxicated driver. The Americans caught up to the drunk, yelling at him to pull over. In reply, the man threw a beer bottle which dented the side of Patrick's car. A few miles later, the two cars pulled alongside each other at a traffic light and Hughes and Silk got out of the car, hockey sticks in hand and hammered away at the drunk's automobile. When they got back in the car, Hughes turned to Silk and calmly asked him if he preferred a Christian or Northland, two makes of hockey sticks, for such work. "I just couldn't believe it," says one player. "I was scared. I got back to my apartment and turned off all the lights and hid." The next night, before the second Canadian game (which the Americans won 6-0), Silk walked around the locker room jokingly claiming that there was a gentleman in the hall looking for a bunch of guys that had dented his car.

The team developed one superstition over the many months on the road. Goalie Jim Craig was required to lead the team out of the locker room, with Harrington next in line. Mike Eruzione had to be the last one out. The players thought these placings brought them luck. Even when the team queued-up to accept their gold medals months later in Lake Placid, the line-up was the same.

One of the major components of Brooks' plan was the demanding schedule the U.S. team had against pro teams, especially those from the Central Hockey League, a minor league proving ground for the NHL. Brooks wanted the pros to go all out against the Olympians, rather than just going through the motions, so he convinced CHL president Bud Poile that all such contests count in the league standings. The games made a big difference in how this club and previous U.S. teams tuned up for the Olympics.

"In the past, our teams took college players and played against college teams in preparation for the Games." says Patrick, assistant coach and captain of the 1979 U.S. national team. "Herb felt to get them ready we had to play better competition. So we stepped almost totally out of college to pro and international teams."

The result was that the Americans played more games in a shorter period of time than most professional teams. During one stretch in early November, they played five games in eight days, all on the road. The team began the week in Houston against the Apollos in a CHL game. The next night they were in Alabama playing the Birmingham Bulls, and then they headed off to the East Coast to take on

Harvard and RPI. They finished the stretch in Cincinnati, against the CHL Stingers. Although Brooks rarely mentioned it, another reason for the large number of exhibition games was to keep the team out of the red. The club received $150,000 from the United States Olympic Committee, but needed nearly $700,000 more to stay solvent. About $200,000 were raised through private contributions, the remainder—some $350,000—had to be made up on the road in gate receipts.

"It's likely that the team is playing some extra games that it would just as soon skip," said Charlie Holt, New Hampshire coach, after the team returned from Europe to begin its North American trek.

The combination of Brooks' desire to play top-flight competition and the USOC's insistence the team stay in the black took its toll, too. The team lost several key players with injuries. Defenseman Jack O'Callahan and forward Dave Silk were both out of the line-up for several games with knee injuries, and defenseman Bob Suter broke his ankle when his skate got stuck in a crack in the ice.

Even with the injuries, the U.S. team played well—winning 15 of 16 games (from mid-October to mid-November). Former Wisconsin star Mark Johnson was the team's leading scorer, earning the nickname "Magic" from his teammates. His linemate, Rob McClanahan, seemed to play better with each game and at one point tallied 12 goals and six assists in only 10 games. The club's impressive record continued until the Americans' four-game rematch with Canada in late November. A few days before the series, Mike Eruzione, just voted captain by his teammates, ran into Eric Strobel in practice. The collision broke Eruzione's left hand. With their captain watching from the stands, the U.S. team suffered four consecutive losses. The Canadians won the first game, scoring with only nine seconds left in the game. The goal disheartened the Americans and they lost the next three games by scores of 6-2, 4-3 and 2-1. "I wouldn't say that we were blown out," says goalie Craig. "All those games were close, except one. I don't really know what happened, we just lost. That was something we weren't used to."

"We weren't really down after those games." adds Christian, "but looking back on it that was probably the low point of the season. I don't know what the problem was."

The team returned to Burnsville, and, for the first time in many weeks, they had a few days off. During free days in the fall, a group of players—Bill Baker, Steve Janaszak, Buzz Schneider, Mike Ramsey and Phil Verchota—spent their time hunting. Baker and Janaszak were the marksmen of the bunch, Schneider and Ramsey the novices, and Verchota tagged along to take pictures. The crew drove out

PHOTO BY PHIL VERCHOTA

Bill Baker (left) and back-up goalie Bruce Horsch out hunting in the Minnesota cornfields.

to the cornfields, one morning after practice, for an adventure resembling a Tom and Jerry cartoon.

As the players stood talking near the cars, Baker spotted a flock of pheasants take off from a neighboring field. He ran off in the direction of the birds, Janaszak right behind him and the others struggling to keep up. Baker had already bagged several birds when Ramsey caught up—minus his gun. He ran back to the car and returned minutes later, only to find that he had forgotten his shells. Meanwhile, Schneider was aiming at anything that flew, and shot several hens, illegal hunting targets. ("Buzzy never could tell colors apart at high speeds," Baker says.) Finally, with the sky clear of any pheasants, Ramsey showed up ready for action. He loaded his gun, aimed at nothing in particular and fired. The force of the blast knocked him backwards, and he tripped over Schneider and fell to the ground.

Upon the team's return to Burnsville, at the end of November, the hunters had a cook-out at the apartment complex. Schneider's wife, Gayle, baked a turkey, and Baker cooked the pheasant, making sure all the Boston players, especially Silk, got a taste of the Minnesota delicacy. "That's the kind of things I remember most about training for the Olympics." Schneider says. "Getting along with the guys so well and the good times we had."

When winter arrived, the wilderness expeditions continued with Baker and Steve Christoff taking their teammates out to Prior Lake, about seven miles from Burnsville, for some ice fishing. Christoff usually came equipped with a bottle of Jack Daniels to ward off the cold. On one such trip, Schneider put down his pole to stretch his legs. Moments later, he heard a splash and turned around to see his rod disappear under the water. From then on, he was famous as the fisherman who went fishing and got caught by the fish.

Another time, Eruzione accompanied Baker for an afternoon of ice fishing in the sub-zero weather. "I told him to dress warm," Baker recalls, "and he shows up wearing a windbreaker and a baseball cap. I put a stocking cap and a sweater in my coat and we left. The first half-hour we're out there and he's saying 'I'm all right, I'm all right.' But an hour later, he was asking for the extra clothes."

PHOTO BY PHIL VERCHOTA

John Harrington at Prior Lake.

In December, the American team rebounded from its losses to Canada and defeated Cincinnati, North Dakota and Yale, but they again lost a game on a late goal. The Adirondack Red Wings of the American Hockey League defeated the U.S., 1-0, scoring with 37 seconds left in the game. The contest was another irritating loss, but there was a bright spot. Brooks had shifted forward Dave Christian to defense for the game, and he performed well. The last time Christian had played defense was in bantam hockey at the age of 16. Despite this, Brooks liked what he saw and kept Christian at the blue line for the rest of the exhibition season and through the Olympics.

There comes a time when a team begins to play as well as it possibly can. Passing plays that have been worked on over and over again in practice succeed for the first time in games. A team suddenly becomes victorious over foes it has previously lost to. And momentum, the intangible that sports people talk about, seems to be on your side. The U.S. Olympic club reached this pinnacle of play during the Pre-Olympic Tournament, held the week before Christmas at Lake Placid. The Americans defeated Sweden, 4-2, decisively subdued Canada, 3-1, and shut out Czechoslovakia, 3-0, to reach the tourney finals against the Soviet Union.

During the tournament, the U.S. had a Christmas party at the hotel. Names were picked out of a hat, and gifts secretly bought. Goalie Jim Craig received a chunk of jawbreaker candy and ear plugs because of his incessant talking about his philosophy of goalkeeping. A note attached to the gift told him to put the jawbreaker in his mouth and hand the ear plugs to those around him when he began a conversation. Mike Eruzione and Eric Strobel received helmets with flashlights taped to the top. The note said the new head gear would help them stay out of each other's way on the ice. Ralph Cox and John Harrington got seat cushions because they were spending a lot of time on the bench. Bill Baker, one of the team's more promising pro prospects, received a toy Corvette with a card saying, "This will have to do for now, until you sign your big-league contract."

Even though the Americans had fun at the tournament, they needed to beat the Soviet Union in their last contest before they could claim first place. The Russian team was a group of second-stringers, and only a handful were named to the national team which competed two months later at the Olympics. But Brooks wanted to show that his system of American hockey could defeat the Soviets, and he figured no time was better than the present. In an exciting contest, the Americans came from behind in the last period to clinch a 5-3 victory. Afterwards the Lake Placid Olympic Committee held medal ceremonies to honor the athletes. The U.S. players walked to the top of the podium and accepted their medals. The last one to receive his award was U.S. captain Mike Eruzione, and at the conclusion of the national anthem he signaled for his teammates to join him atop the victory platform. They simply waved and skated off the ice.

As the crowd filed out of the arena and into the bars across the street, the question heard over and over was "Could they do it again?" At the post-game press conference, Rob McClanahan angrily answered a reporter who voiced the same question. "That's a stupid thing to ask." he said. "If I didn't think we could win the gold medal, I wouldn't be here."

Most players on the U.S. team wanted to jump the calendar ahead six weeks after the finish in the Pre-Olympic Tournament. They had only three days off, and many flew back and saw their families for the first time in months. The day after Christmas, they were back on the road, this time in Omaha, Nebraska, playing Gorki Torpedo, another Russian "B" team. The Americans won the game and the next two against Russian opponents. However, the team began to lose its edge. It became complacent on defense and its adversaries, instead of scoring one or two goals a game, were now averaging nearly three. The team shut out only one opponent, the Warroad Lakers, in Warroad, Minnesota, during January. Before their slump, the club had had eight shut-outs.

"We came out of that Pre-Olympic Tournament and a lot of guys just went, 'Jeez, we've got 15 games in January still to play' " John Harrington says. "We just wanted to get through those games and get back to Lake Placid. We probably weren't preparing as hard as we should have for those games, but there were so many of them, four a week sometimes, and it just got to the point where you said, 'Do we have to go out and play again tonight?'"

In the U.S. team press releases, coach Brooks said his team was "starting to peak at the right time." Actually, he was worried about his squad's play and, less than three weeks before the Olympics, he decided to shake his team up. The move almost backfired.

Since the July try-outs in Colorado Springs, Brooks had kept several college players like Craig Homola of Vermont, Donny Waddell of Northern Michigan and Tim Harrer and Aaron Broten of Minnesota, listed as Olympic back-ups. With his team playing poorly Brooks announced the reserves would receive new trials with the U.S. club. The players already on the Olympic traveling team reacted bitterly.

"The thing we questioned was 'Why now'?" Eruzione says. "Why only a couple of weeks before the games? Aaron Broten may have taken my job away from me if I hadn't gotten going. But we felt that you can't bring a guy in for a game against the Warroad Lakers and then tell him he's won a job. We wanted them to play five games in eight nights like we had been doing."

The players had a team meeting, and told Brooks, through assistant coach Patrick and captain Eruzione, to drop his idea of bringing in college back-ups. Brooks finally agreed, even though Tim Harrer did play in four games.

"I made a mistake," Brooks admits. "If I was going to do anything with those back-up players I should have done it earlier. I waited too long.

"I talked with Eruzione and Patrick about it and decided that, all right, you want to be a family, we've been a family and we're staying that way. It worked."

Looking back on the incident, it's possible that bringing in the college players was another of Brooks' efforts to rouse his team. "Who knows?" says Harrington. "I'm sure he'll never say. It's another thing he did that may have been a mistake, but it worked out. He's got the curse of success."

Even with the tension, the U.S. team still had time for mirth and merriment. For instance, on a plane from Dallas to Minneapolis the players had no room underneath their seats to set their cowboy hats. Several players, led by Harrington and Christian, put their hats on empty seats in the first-class section. During the flight, the stewardess told the pair they owed the airline $7,000 for placing unauthorized luggage in the first-class section. After arguing with them, she demanded to know who was the team's coach. Christian pointed to Eruzione. The stewardess stormed up to the captain, berating him about the players' conduct. Eruzione, trying to figure out what was going on, apologized and told her he would take care of the matter. Behind the stewardess' back, Harrington had retrieved his hat and was passing it among the regular passengers, mockingly trying to raise the necessary funds. They played along with Harrington's prank, throwing rings, wallets, necklaces and money clips into his hat. When the stewardess saw the proceedings she ordered Eruzione to move the hats and retreated from the coach section to a chorus of boos from the team and the passengers.

As the exhibition season drew to a close in late January, Brooks had to decide what players he was to cut. He had already dropped Les Auge, Dave Delich and Bruce Horsch from the team, and Gary Ross had retired. Each cut had been an agonizing process, especially in the case of Auge. "I recruited him, he was from my neighborhood, he works for me in my hockey school," Brooks says. "So if I had one close friend on that team going into the year it was Les Auge. That killed me to cut him."

Two more players had to be dropped and the unlucky pair were Jack Hughes, a defenseman from Harvard, and Ralph Cox, an All-American forward from New Hampshire. Hughes and Cox found out about the coach's decision only hours before they were supposed to attend a send-off banquet for the team in Minneapolis. The

PHOTO COURTESY OF VOLKSWAGEN

Another press conference on the road. Coach Herb Brooks being interviewed while the team looks on. During the Olympics, Brooks refused to allow his players to talk at press conferences. From day one, he was the team's coach and only spokesman.

two went to the dinner and consoled each other over beer. "I wasn't bitter, but I felt some pain," Cox, the top 1979 college scorer nationwide, remembers. "I was a part of a the team. I went through all the difficult times with them. But I never got the chance to share in the best times. I felt like I should have been with them up in Lake Placid."

Before going on to Lake Placid, the U.S. team had one more exhibition game—against the Russian Olympic team, considered by many to be the best in the world. Neither team had much to gain by the contest since it would not count in the Olympic standings. The game more than likely was arranged by the USOC to help the American team pay its bills.

A large crowd packed Madison Square Garden in New York that afternoon for the contest. The Afghanistan crisis and Iranian hostages fresh in their minds, many attended in the hopes of seeing the Russian horde beaten. In the locker room before the game, Brooks told his players that this was "the last game of spring training," and he did not display his usual confidence or enthusiasm. His team was trounced by the Soviets, 10-3. The Americans kept up to the Russians for only a half-period of play. After the game, a Soviet team spokesman accused the U.S. of "holding back." Brooks chided the New York press for being gloomy about his team's chances at Lake Placid. "This isn't a wake," he said, after admitting that he had not properly prepared his team for the contest. Later that afternoon, captain Mike Eruzione went out with his family to Toots Shor, a fashionable nightspot. The captain was in high spirits despite the loss, maintaining that the U.S. team learned a great lesson that afternoon. He even predicted that the Americans would defeat the Soviet team at Lake Placid. Nobody at the table believed him.

CHAPTER 2

Going for the Gold

They have the spirit. You can almost touch it.
—Finn coach Frank Moberg, commenting on
the U.S. hockey team.

The evening sky was overcast and revealed no stars the night the U.S. team left New York and boarded a plane bound for Lake Placid, some 275 miles to the north. On the flight, captain Eruzione talked with many of his teammates, convincing them the Russian loss was not the end of the world, and that they would do much better the second time around. The team arrived in Lake Placid, feeling a little more confident. "They were still emotionally low," remembers Peter Rush, the team's Olympic host. "But guys like Mike Eruzione, Jim Craig, Mark Johnson were getting everybody excited about playing in the Olympics. That Eruzione, he was incredible. I think he was born to be the captain of that team."

During the first 10 days of the Olympics, each team played the others within its division once, and then the top two teams advanced to the final round, with a chance of winning a medal. The U.S. club was in a six-team league called the Blue Division with Sweden, Czechoslovakia, West Germany, Norway and Romania. In the other Olympic hockey league, the Red Division, the Soviet Union was expected to go undefeated into the medal round. Finland, Japan, Canada and Poland would battle it out for second place.

The Americans' first two games of the tournament were against Sweden and Czechoslovakia, the two seeds in the Blue Division. Since September, Brooks had emphasized the importance of these two games. The Swedes were favored to win the bronze and the Czechs were expected to challenge the Russians for the gold. Brooks warned his team repeatedly that a defeat to either the Swedes or the Czechs would be costly, and to lose to both would put the Americans swiftly out of the medal picture.

TUESDAY, FEBRUARY 12, SWEDEN

The opening ceremonies were still a day away when the U.S. took on Sweden. The arena—which a week later would be packed with sell-out crowds—was only half-full tonight. As a country, Sweden is known for producing quality skaters and some of its best players,

PHOTO BY PETE HALPERN

The Americans surround a Soviet shooter.

like Borje Salming, Ulf Nilsson and Anders Hedberg, have gone onto careers in the NHL. However, the Swedes often rely too much on individual talent and rarely mold their skilled players into a team. The 1980 team had only six practices together before the Olympics. Asked what tactics his club intended to use against Brooks' brand of American hockey, Swedish coach Bengt Ohlson rolled his eyes and said, "Systems? We don't have time for that."

Even with no planned attack, the Swedes were still favored over the Americans. Sweden had four fleet lines and a brilliant goal-keeper in Pelle Lindbergh, a second-round choice of the Philadel-phia Flyers in the 1979 NHL draft.

Meanwhile, the U.S. was in trouble at the blue line. The club was down to four defensemen. Jack O'Callahan, the team's most mobile back-liner, had injured his knee for the second time in four months in the Russian exhibition game at Madison Square Garden. Many doubted that he would play at all in the Olympics. Bob Suter, who had broken his ankle during the exhibition season, was in uniform, but was not playing well. That left coach Brooks with the defensive pairings of Morrow-Ramsey and Christian-Baker. The foursome would have to play virtually the entire game.

From the opening face-off, the game settled into a battle of the goalies. Although U.S. netminder Craig had had a miserable time

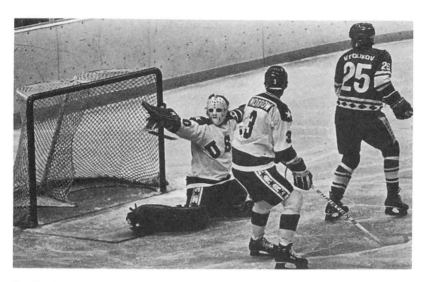

Goalie Jim Craig stops the Russians.

during the team's January slump, tonight he was sparkling, and at
the other end of the ice Sweden's Lindbergh was just as outstanding. The teams took turns moving the puck up and down the ice,
only to be stopped time after time by either goalie. Like a pitchers'
duel in baseball, such battles are usually decided by breaks, mistakes and a few key plays.

Craig made 17 saves in the first period, but Sweden scored the
first goal of the game on a nice, three-way passing play midway
through the first period. Minutes later, Rob McClanahan was
slammed into the boards by a Swede. He limped to the locker room,
suffering from a charley horse. U.S. trainer Bruce Kola thought the
injury serious enough to keep the U.S. forward out of the rest of the
game. But Brooks had other thoughts. At the end of the first period,
with his team trailing, 1-0, he stormed into the locker room and
began shouting at his players. Noticing McClanahan with his skates
off, Brooks ordered him to get dressed and to be back on the bench
for the next period. The pair launched into a shouting match. "You
can take your team and shove it!" McClanahan told Brooks at one
point. The U.S. coach had to be restrained by Jack O'Callahan.
Cooler heads prevailed, though, and McClanahan was back in uniform for the next period. The incident aroused the U.S. team, and in
the second period the Americans began to outplay the Swedes.
"You can say we rallied behind both of them." says captain Eruzione.
"It was a big thing for the team."

The Americans tested Lindbergh, but failed to put the puck by him until there were only 28 seconds left in the second period. Dave Silk and Mark Johnson broke in over the Sweden blue line, momentarily running into each other, before Silk shot the puck into the net. The play typified the U.S. effort that night—excited, determined and slightly out of control. The Americans were often out of position, and Brooks' team concept was frequently forgotten, with each player trying to do everything by himself.

The game was tied, 1-1, in the third period when Brooks gambled and lost. Realizing his defense was exhausted, he put Bob Suter in for a shift. Twenty seconds later, the Swedes scored as the Americans became confused in their own end and Suter did not move his man out from in front of the net. The goal by Thomas Eriksson looked insurmountable as Lindbergh held off the U.S. attack. With 41 seconds left in the game, Brooks pulled Craig in favor of an extra forward. The U.S. net was unguarded and the American players crowded into the Sweden end, looking for the tying goal. Buzz Schneider got hold of the puck in the corner and passed it in the direction of Johnson, who was breaking for the net. Two Swedish defensemen converged on Johnson and the puck slid through to defenseman Bill Baker at the blue line. Without stopping the puck, Baker shot a low, 55-foot drive into the net to tie the game at 2-2, and that's the way it ended. The goal came with only 27 seconds left in the game and was Baker's only point of the Olympics.

"I had a lot of chances throughout the Olympics, but that was my only goal." he remembers. "Schneider fed me a great pass. I didn't signal or yell to him, we just made eye contact for a brief second and then the pass was coming my way. The defensemen had caved in on Mark, so I had plenty of room. I was just trying to get it on net."

THURSDAY, FEBRUARY 14, CZECHOSLOVAKIA

Most teams would have been nervous before a game against the Czechs. After all, they were the No. 2 team in the tournament, and the Americans had to win if they wanted to remain in a tie for first place. The Czechs saw the game as a chance to put the Americans behind them in the standings. But the U.S. team was relaxed and laughing before the Czech game; Dave Christian made sure of that. The forward-turned-defenseman arrived early in the locker room, and using tape, cardboard and a coat hanger, he fashioned a pair of wings and a tail for his helmet. He then got dressed and sat in his stall as his teammates walked in, staring at his new hat. While they suited up, Christian announced, "Guys, something tells me that I'm really going to fly tonight." The room broke up.

The Czechs opened the scoring at 2:23 of the first period on a goal by Jaroslav Pouzar. Eruzione tied the game minutes later. The Iron Rangers—the line of Buzz Schneider, John Harrington and Mark Pavelich—scored next, with Pavelich putting the puck in. And Marian Stastny of Czechoslovakia tied the game, the assist going to his brother, Peter.

The Americans took the lead for good in the second period as Pavelich and Schneider combined on a pretty passing play. Spinning away from a Czech defenseman, Pavelich backhanded a pass across the crease to Schneider, who deflected it into the net. Mark Johnson then stickhandled in on the Czech goalie, leaving a defenseman flat-footed in his wake, and lifted a backhand into the net. After two periods, the U.S. led, 4-2.

Going into the third period with a two-goal lead over a powerful team like the Czechs, a veteran squad would have played it safe. However, with the crowd cheering them on, the young Americans got carried away and completely outplayed their rivals. "I think that may have been the best game we played all year, better than the game against Russia," says Jack O'Callahan. "I can't remember us ever being better than that night."

The U.S. goals came in fast succession. Dave Christian rushed down the ice and was checked off the puck and into Czech goalkeeper Jiri Kralik. Phil Verchota knocked the loose puck into the net. The Iron Rangers struck again. Schneider scored his second goal of the game, after Harrington passed him the puck in front of the Czech goal. After a Czech goal, Johnson raced through center ice and passed the puck to McClanahan. As he sprawled on the ice, McClanahan lifted the puck into the net.

The Czechs were angry at the U.S. for running up the score and with two minutes left in the game, a Czech defenseman axed Johnson across the shoulder with his stick. The American center fell to the ice, and was carried into the locker room.

"I thought I had dislocated it. I was in a great deal of pain," Johnson says. "I found out that night, after they x-rayed it, that it wasn't dislocated and nothing was broken, so I was going to play. It just meant putting up with some pain—it was a nagging kind of pain. When I got checked on it, there was a sharp pain, but most of the time it just ached."

The fans, though, quickly forgot about Johnson's injury and when Craig caught a Czech shot with his glove and held it aloft at the final buzzer, the crowd stood and applauded. On Valentine's Day 1980, America found a new bunch of sweethearts.

SATURDAY, FEBRUARY 16, NORWAY

The stunning victory over Czechoslovakia kept the Americans deadlocked with Sweden for first place in the Blue Division. The U.S. team now found itself in a new dilemma. They were no longer underdogs for their upcoming contests against Norway, Romania and West Germany. Brooks worried that his team might have a let-down. In practice he repeated one of his slogans, telling them that they weren't talented enough to win on talent alone. The remark insulted several players.

The Norway game took place in the old arena, an ancient structure that seated less than 2,000 spectators. The U.S. team must have imagined they were back on the road in some small rink against a minor-league opponent because in the first period, they were sluggish. Too many of their passes were off target. Norway, meanwhile, was playing about as well as it could. Routed by the West Germany and the Czechs, it was determined not to be embarrassed against the U.S. Norway scored the only goal of the opening period on a power play. A shot by Geir Myhre sailed over Craig's shoulder and into the net. After the first period, the Americans sat in the locker room, trying to regain their composure. Silk made a speech suggesting that everyone say nice things to each other, and for the rest of the intermission, the players complimented each other on their hair styles, eye color and how they put on their equipment. The nonsense brought results. Eruzione scored an unassisted goal only 41 seconds into the new stanza. Craig then made a big stop on a breakaway by Stephen Fronst, and Johnson and Silk finished out the scoring in the period. Former Bowling Green teammates Mark Wells and Ken Morrow scored in the third period.

Even though the U.S. had won handily, 5-1, Brooks was dissatisfied. "I better take the whip to these guys." he said after the game. "Some of them are backing up to the pay window."

MONDAY, FEBRUARY 18, ROMANIA

Defenseman Jack O'Callahan returned to the line-up and his arrival woke up his teammates.

The Iron Rangers scored the first goal of the game at 12:03. The trio broke down ice and crossed the Romanian blue line. Pavelich, on the right side, dropped the puck back to Harrington. Just as he was about to be checked, Harrington slid the puck back to Pavelich, who passed it cross ice to a speeding Schneider. The Romanian goalie had no chance as Schneider deflected it into the net.

Eric Strobel scored his only Olympic goal minutes later as he stickhandled in front of the Romanian net, waiting until the goalie and two defensemen lunged at him. With their bodies sprawled in front of the net, Strobel calmly lifted the puck high into the nets. Both goals, one a team effort, the other an individual feat, were among the most graceful goals of the tournament.

Mark Wells, Steve Christoff, and Rob McClanahan also scored as the U.S. won, 7-2. O'Callahan even got into the act, collecting an assist on Christoff's goal.

WEDNESDAY, FEBRUARY 20, WEST GERMANY

In the 1976 Olympics, the U.S. hockey team seemingly had a bronze medal in its grasp, when all they had to do was defeat or tie West Germany to secure a third-place finish. The U.S. lost the game, 4-1, and ever since, American-West German hockey contests have been grudge matches. The Team's 1980 confrontation continued the pattern. Twenty-four minutes in penalties were called, and several times the players almost came to blows. The U.S. did not have to win the game to advance to the medal round. Earlier in the day, Sweden had beaten Czechoslovakia, so the Americans and the Swedes would represent the Blue Division in the medal round. Despite this, the U.S. wanted to win this game.

"We wanted it because of pride, prestige and to keep our momentum going," says Schneider, a member of the 1976 U.S. Olympic team. "The West Germans were upset because they hadn't had a good Olympics, but they've always been a team that in the past has given American teams trouble, and that was on the players' mind.

"I wanted to beat them especially bad because of '76. You'd think something like that won't bother you, that you'd forget it. But I hadn't."

The West Germans opened up a 2-0 lead in the first period. U.S. goals by McClanahan and Neal Broten evened the score after two periods. McClanahan scored again in the third period and Phil Verchota got the final goal and the U.S. had a 4-2 victory. At the conclusion of the game, the medal pairings were announced: Sweden would play Finland and the U.S. would face off against Russia on Friday.

FRIDAY, FEBRUARY 22, RUSSIA

The last time the Soviet Union had lost an Olympic championship was 1960, and the Russians had not lost a game in Olympic hockey since 1968. However, throughout this tournament they looked vul-

Forward-turned-defenseman Dave Christian rides a Russian out of the play in front of the U.S. bench.

nerable. The Finns had the Russians on the ropes, ahead 2-1 in the third period. But with 15 minutes left, the Finns began to ice the puck and play defensively. The Soviets then struck for three goals in less than two minutes to pull out a 4-2 win. The Canadians were leading the Soviet Union, 4-3, in the last period when Aleksandre Gloikov scored three goals, including two in 12 seconds. Many of the American players watched the games and slowly the word spread—the Soviets could be beaten. "They looked slow sometimes," says Eric Strobel. "We thought they were a bit too old."

Indeed, the age of the Russians' top line of Kharlamov-Petrov-Mikhailov totaled 99 years, compared to the total age of 66 years for the American line of McClanahan-Johnson-Silk. Eight Soviets were on the Russian squad that stunned the world by defeating Team Canada in 1972. That year, 12 members of the U.S. club were still playing pee wee hockey.

The Americans were ready, and nobody was more excited about the prospect of dethroning the Russians than goalie Craig. The day before the game, he confidently told coach Brooks that "We're going to do it. Just watch." Later, Craig admitted that he had been rooting for the Soviets in their contests with Finland and Canada. "If anyone beat them, I wanted it to be us." he said.

Bill Cleary, a member of the 1960 U.S. team, visited the Americans before the game. After he left, Brooks entered the locker room, pulled out another crumpled piece of yellow paper and read his team a new message. "You were born to be a player. You were meant for this moment," he said. "You were meant to be here. So let's have poise and possession of ourselves at this time."

In the early moments of the game, about the only one who remembered Brooks' pep talk was Craig. The U.S. goalie made several outstanding saves as the American defense had problems moving the puck out of its zone. Near the nine-minute mark, Schneider circled his own net with the puck, but was checked by a Russian. The puck came loose to Aleksei Kasatonov, and his slapshot was deflected past Craig by Vladimir Krutov.

On Schneider's next shift on the ice, he atoned for his mistake. Taking a pass from Pavelich, he powered a slapshot over Vladislav Tretyak's glove and into the net. "I had a lot of time and Pav gave me a good pass." Schneider remembers. "I thought that if I could catch him on the glove side someplace, it would go in. I didn't know if it was going to be low or high. He was moving a little bit to the right and as soon as I looked up after letting it go I could tell that it was good. Boy, to blow one by him from that far out is something. I couldn't believe it."

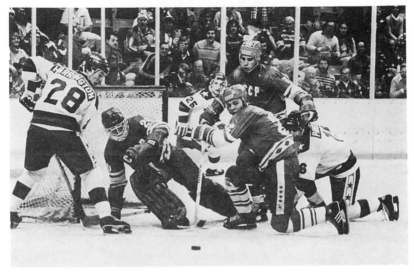

PHOTO BY L.P.O.O.C.

The Iron Rangers (Pavelich, Harrington and Schneider) storm the Soviet goal and Russian net minder Vladislav Tretyak, scrambles to make the save.

Craig kept the U.S. tied with the Soviets until Sergei Makarov scored on a pass from Vladimir Golikov at 17:34. The period looked like it would end with the Russians ahead 2-1, but Christian launched a 100-foot slapshot at Tretyak. The Russian goalie made the save, However, the rebound slithered out to Johnson. The U.S. center grabbed the loose puck, faked Tretyak out of position, and scored with one second remaining.

"I went right in between two Russian defensemen after the puck," Johnson says "That surprised me. It was like they thought the period was over, they weren't awake. When I got to the puck the time element went totally out of my mind. I was thinking only about putting it in. Probably if I had thought about the time I would have just shot it right away. After I put it in, I looked up at the scoreboard and there were three big zeros there and I just thought I had screwed up."

The goal stood and the Americans had a 2-2 tie after one period.

"That sent us into the locker room on cloud nine rather than being a goal behind." O'Callahan says. "Instead of them going in a goal up and laughing, and us down a goal and worrying, we're tied and the Russians are beginning to doubt themselves. That's quite a turnabout, and things like that just don't happen naturally. It's almost like the parting of the Red Sea.

Top: *Mike Eruziones' shot rolls through the crease.* Middle: *Mark Johnson ties the score at 2-2 as the first period ends.* Bottom: *Russian goalie Vladislav Tretyak looks back at the puck.*

Top r.: *Mike Ramsey moves in to clear loose puck from in front of U.S. net.* Top l.: *Defenseman Ken Morrow mixes it up with a Russian.* Middle: *Morrow knocks Valeri Kharlamov to the ice.* Bottom: *Another incredible save by Jim Craig. Mark Pavelich looks on.*

Aleksandr Maltsev gives the Russians their last lead of the game, 3-2, in the second period.

The only goal of the second period belonged to Russia's Alexsandr Maltsev, as he split the U.S. defense and scored easily on Craig. For a moment, it seemed that it was all over for the Americans. The defense again looked shaky and the Russians moved in for the kill. But Craig turned aside several Soviet shots and his teammates rebounded. Even though he was beaten by several long shots, Craig came up with the big save throughout the Olympics. Against North American goalies, the Russians usually score easy goals by faking the netminder and then passing the puck around him to a teammate who puts it in the open net. "Fake once and move around him. Bang. It is easy," said a spokesman from Tass, the Russian news agency before the game. "We believe the same tactic will work against Craig." But the U.S. goalie had learned his lesson in the 10-3 loss to the Russians at Madison Square Garden. Now, Craig stayed back in his net, on his feet waiting for the Soviets to make the first move.

The Americans tied the score at 8:39 of the third period. Silk, with McClanahan and Johnson on the wings, carried the puck into the Soviet zone. He was hip-checked to the ice but not before he pushed the puck ahead. Silk's weak shot hit a Russian skate and bounced out to the ever-opportunistic Johnson. He put it past the new Soviet goalie Vladimir Myshkin. Eighty-one seconds later, the impossible became reality as Eruzione scored the go-ahead goal for the Americans.

"Pavelich somehow bounded the puck past the defenseman, and I picked it up." Eruzione says. "I shot off the wrong foot and it went in. But, as I said to a couple of friends, of all the goals I've scored in my life where I didn't know what was going on, I knew exactly what I was doing then. I knew either the (Russian) defenseman had to come at me and if that happened I'd give it to Baker, or the defenseman would go down and try to block the shot. He tried doing that

PHOTOS BY PETE HALPERN

Top: *Neal Broten and Mike Eruzione in front of Russian goal.* Bottom: *The American bench mobs Mike Eruzione after his goal puts the U.S. ahead to stay, 4-3, against the Soviets.*

and I used him as a screen. It went by him and I don't think the goalie saw it either.''

Up in the stands, Eugene and Helen Eruzione were sitting with Wisconsin coach Bob Johnson and his wife, Martha. After the Johnsons' son Mark tied the game, Mr. Eruzione said to his wife, ''Helen, Mike hasn't done anything yet.'' Moments later, their son scored and the quartet jumped up and down, hugging each other. Martha Johnson lost an earring and Mr. Eruzione's glasses were knocked off in the celebration.

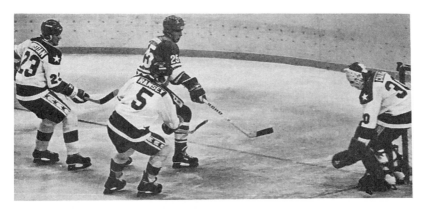

PHOTOS BY PETE HALPERN

Clockwise from top: *Dave Christian and Mike Ramsey force Russian to take shot from bad angle; the U.S. attack starts down ice; John Harrington of the Iron Rangers closes in on man with puck; Neal Broten moves in on Russian defense; Phil Verchota passes the puck out of his own zone.*

PHOTOS BY PETE HALPERN
Top l.: *The Iron Rangers buzz around Soviet goal.* Right: *Dave Christian tangles with Soviet player.* Bottom l.: *Mike Ramsey blocks a shot.*

There were 10 minutes left to play, and the Russians began changing lines every 45 seconds in an effort to catch the fatigued Americans off-guard. The U.S. team scrambled to stay in control of the game, something the Finns and the Canadians had failed to do in their near upsets of the Soviets. "I must have said at least 100 Hail Marys in the last 10 minutes." says Mrs. Eruzione. On the American bench the sentiments were the same. "I was shaking and everybody was nervous because you never know what can happen." Schneider says. "The puck could go off somebody's skate and they could tie it up again. We were hanging on, nobody could believe it.

"It was one of those games that you think is eight or nine hours long. You got to thinking, When is this thing going to end? It just kept going back and forth."

The Russians came close to tying the game. However, each time the Americans began playing defensively, a mistake Canada and Finland had made, Brooks pulled those players off the ice and replaced them with a new line. "Play your game. Play your game." he told them on the bench. The tactic worked and the Russians, not the U.S., lost their poise as they began shooting the puck in. "We just played 60 minutes of good hockey," Eruzione says. "In the last five minutes they panicked."

Finally, the final seconds elapsed on the scoreboard its face reading U.S. -4, C.C.C.P. -3 and America had scored the biggest upset in hockey history.

Sticks and gloves flew in the air as the U.S. bench emptied to congratulate goalie Craig. The team came together in a jumping, hugging, smiling pile of humanity near the U.S. net. The crowd of 10,000 shouted "USA! USA!" and the roar was probably heard at the Canadian boarder, 45 miles to the north. It was one of those rare moments when an underdog not only puts up a good battle but wins the game. Forget the Dallas Cowboys or the New York Yankees. This was America's Team.

The victory celebration spilled out onto Main Street and soon Lake Placid was jammed with fans shouting "We're No. 1" and drinking toasts to the hockey team. An hour and half later the celebration was still going on as the U.S. bus moved through the throng slowly making its way back to the Olympic village. On board, the team was singing "God Bless America."

PHOTO BY L.P.O.O.C.

The celebration begins moments after the final buzzer sounds with the U.S. 4-3 winners over the Soviet Union.

SUNDAY, FEBRUARY 26, FINLAND

Cheers of "USA! USA!" still seemed to echo down Main Street on that cold morning. The Finland-U.S. contest was due to begin at 11 a.m., a time everyone agreed was too early. If the U.S. won, America had the gold.* During the 39 hours since the Russian upset, the U.S. locker room had been flooded with telegrams from across the country. One read "Congratulations for kicking the Soviet butts. What's your secret? The Afghan Rebels." The Americans were at ease as the game began, and, predictably, they fell behind.

Jukka Porvari scored and Finland had a 1-0 lead. The tally marked the sixth time in seven games the U.S. trailed, and, as before, the Americans would have to come from behind to win. The U.S. got on the scoreboard when Steve Christoff stole the puck from a Finnish defenseman and put a weak backhand on net. The slowness of the shot surprised Finnish goalie Jorma Valtonen and the puck slipped in between his pads and rolled into the net. Finland again went on top as Mikko Leinonen scored on a power play. The second period ended with the U.S. losing, 2-1.

"We weren't nervous in the locker room" says John Harrington. "We had come back before and we expected it from ourselves." By now, so had a nation.

The U.S. squad was in almost the same position the 1960 club had been in: down a goal entering the last period of the final game. The 1960 team needed a victory over Czechoslovakia and found themselves losing 4-3. The 1960 team won that game and one of the leaders of that comeback was Billy Christian. Twenty years later, his son, Dave, rose to the occasion. Two and half minutes into the third period, he sped through the Finnish defense and passed off to Verchota, who beat Valtonen with a low shot inside the far post.

Less than four minutes later, Johnson and Strobel battled the Finn defensemen for the puck. Johnson gained control and shoveled it out to McClanahan in front of the Finn net. McClanahan waited, and Voltonen, thinking the American winger was aiming for the long side, made his move. McClanahan stuffed the puck in between the goalie's legs.

Although the Americans led 3-2, the tension was far from over. The U.S. received three penalties and only Craig's goaltending and the forechecking of Neal Broten, and Steve Christoff kept the Finns from scoring. During the last American penalty, Broten broke up a Finn rush, and then raced to the bench. Christoff carried on, checking a Finn into the boards and gaining control of the puck. He

---

* For round robin results and final standings—see page 128.

passed it in the direction of Johnson, who had replaced Broten. The 5'9", 155-pound center got the puck, raced in on goal and fired a backhand. A Finn defenseman hit him from behind, causing pain in his injured shoulder, but Johnson retrieved the rebound and slipped the puck into the net.

"I wanted to shoot right away, but the puck was bounding and I had to keep after it, and because of that I went deeper into the zone," Johnson says. "I shot, and the goalie saved it. The rebound was lying there and I put it in. You don't think about defensemen when you're in a spot like that."

The cheering inside the arena swelled to a single roar with 13 seconds left in the game. The fans counted off the final seconds, and the game was over and the gold belonged to America. The U.S. team shook hands with the Finns and then saluted their fans. In living rooms across America, there were smiles, shouts and glistening eyes. A scrappy bunch of young Americans had proved what a little heart and determination can do.

Back in the U.S. locker room, the exhausted players sat down with weary smiles on their faces. There was a knock on the door, and an ABC spokesman poked his head in. "We've set up a special room for you," he said. "Vice-President Mondale is waiting to congratulate you, and the President will be calling." What he failed to mention was ABC was also ready to film the event.

"You want to do that," said captain Eruzione. "Then you can do it right here."

Stunned, the ABC man left and television cameras, lights and telephone hook-ups were soon brought into the locker room. During the delay, ABC's Jim McKay explained to the television audience that the team was still on its way to the locker room. Actually, they were waiting for the technicians to finish their work. Fifteen minutes later, it was lights, camera, action as captain Eruzione talked with the President.

"Tell the team how much I love them and we'll see you tomorrow at the White House," Carter said. "We're all proud of you."

"Thank you very much." Eruzione said. "We'll all be there."

"Good luck," said the President.

"Good luck to you," replied the U.S. captain.

The day after its stunning victory over Finland, the hockey team and the rest of the Olympic squad flew to Washington for a reception with the President and the First Lady. In a speech from the White House steps, Mr. Carter called the athletes "modern-day heroes."

"For me, as President of the United States, this is one of the proudest moments I have ever experienced," he added.

Brooks presented the President with a white stocking Olympic cap. "Going out and seeing Americans as we did today gives us the impression we really did something for all the country." the U.S. coach told reporters. "It gives a little different perspective on what is meant to be an American."

Gazing out over the White House lawn, captain Eruzione remarked, "I'd love to hit a few golf balls on that."

After the Presidential reception, the team began to disband. Ken Morrow, Jim Craig and Mark Johnson signed lucrative pro contracts and left to join their new teams. Meanwhile, the majority of the team moved on, this time to New York City where the Big Apple's boos had turned to cheers. The team that assembled in New York was unsigned as far as NHL contracts were concerned. However, they were also working for a paycheck. The team was in town to film a Volkswagen commercial and to pose for accompanying magazine photographs. The car company flew the Olympians and their wives or dates to New York to do the advertisements.

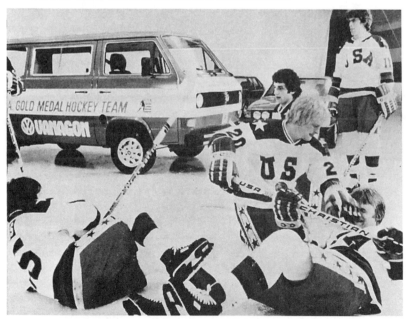

PHOTO COURTESY OF VOLKSWAGEN

Members of U.S. Olympic Hockey Team prior to shooting Volkswagen Vanagon commercial. Shown are (l. to r.): Mark Wells, Bob Suter, Phil Verchota. Also shown (in background) are: Buzz Schneider, and Steve Christoff of U.S. Olympic Hockey Team.

Volkswagen rented out 24 rooms at The Plaza hotel, a luxury establishment across from Central Park, for the Olympic entourage. The prices at the Plaza were extravagent, with a six-ounce orange juice costing $2.95 and an Edwardian, breakfast item resembling a McDonald's Egg McMuffin, going for $9.95. But the players rarely looked at the bottom line—they simply charged the bill to Volkswagen.

Rob McClanahan relaxing in New York City.

For the players from the small towns of Minnesota and Massachusetts, it was an overwhelming experience. Money during their days in New York was everywhere and in some inexperienced hands. Rob McClanahan gave his fiancée a $100 bill to go shopping, but she didn't want to break it. Buying a pack of cigarettes, she came up 15 cents short, and agonized over having to cash in the $100 bill. "I've never seen one of these before," she said. "I don't want to give it up yet." Eventually, she borrowed the 15 cents and held onto the $100.

For the team's first night in New York as heroes, they traveled by limousine to the Roxy Roller Disco in lower Manhatten. Inside, the Olympic stars changed into T-shirts and laced up rented roller skates. "I hope I don't break a leg," said Mike Ramsey. "I haven't signed yet."

Outside the disco, the scene looked like a movie opening. Spectators pressed against police barricades and cheered for anyone they recognized. Japanese television was in attendance, looking for someone from the hockey team to interview. Neither the TV crew or the fans had long to wait as Brooks, hampered by a cold, left the party early.

Through a translator, the Japanese commentator asked Brooks how he felt about his team. "I guess I'm like a father who is very happy for his sons," the coach said. "That's about the only way I can describe it."

Coach Herb Brooks holds up key to the City of New York, as singer Robert Merrill leads the crowd in singing "America the Beautiful." Doing the honors were City Council President Carol Bellamy (right). Also shown is John Harrington (left).

The next morning the team was due to accept the key to New York City at 12:30, but at least one player did not make the trip because of a hangover. The remaining contingent walked onto the speaker's platform at City Hall to the music of the Olympic theme, played by an all-girl high school band decked out in three-cornered hats. Brooks had the spectators cheering as he waved an "I love New York" scarf before taking his seat. The players were introduced, and "The Star-Spangled Banner" and "America the Beautiful" sung. After accepting the key to the city, Brooks told the audience: "Each of the players had a gold medal and it's theirs—they've earned it. But in so many ways that gold medal is yours, too. The medal stands for our system and our way of life, a system that stresses talent, enthusiasm and the work ethic."

Later, on a tour of City Hall, Brooks put the key down. That proved to be his first major mistake in six months. At the tour's conclusion, he went to pick up the key and found it gone. Somebody had stolen it.

PART II
Meet the
Champions

Phil Verchota in Pony League.

PHOTO COURTESY OF THE BAKERS

Bill Baker (middle) and two teammates, Steve Fleming and Jeff Oakley, with the third-place trophy they won at a Pee Wee tournament in Babbitt, Minnesota.

It was· in the small towns and suburbs that the basic traits and characteristics like determination, skill, hard work, patience and enthusiasm were developed. The U.S. hockey team was a blend of such qualities and these virtues were the major reasons behind the team's success. Each important trait was exemplified by at least one athlete on the Olympic roster. Growing up in Charlestown, Massachusetts, taught Jack O'Callahan to be enthusiastic and emotional. More than a thousand miles away in Babbitt, Minnesota, Buzz Schneider learned to be patient, yet determined in his quest to be a hockey player. This section of the book focuses on these players and others like Eric Strobel, John Harrington, Rob McClanahan, Mike Eruzione, Jim Craig and Ken Morrow and what each contributed to the U.S. club. To fully understand the amazing victory at Lake Placid, one must visit these hometowns, talk with family and friends and slowly see the beginnings of a team capable of bringing home the gold.

CHAPTER 3

The Minnesota Way

Years before Rob McClanahan, Neal Broten, Bill Baker, Eric Strobel or any of the other Minnesota Olympians laced up their first pair of skates, the ice was already waiting for them. Clear and smooth, its cracks polished away by the cold Minnesota snow and wind, the neighborhood pond was so close that they only had to put on their skates and walk out the back door to reach it.

Carved by the glaciers, from International Falls to the Twin Cities of Minneapolis and St. Paul, the state of Minnesota is dimpled like the outside of a golf ball. When the glaciers receded millions of years ago, the cavities filled with the melted water and the land of the lakes was born. During the summer Minnesota goes fishing. The state sells more fishing licenses and has more boats per capita than any other state in the Union. In the winter, though, when the average temperature hovers around 20 degrees Fahrenheit, Minnesota freezes like a giant ice cube tray and its favorite sport becomes hockey. At last count, Minnesota had 10,809 lakes more than 25 acres in area, and thousands of smaller bodies of water which serve as hockey playgrounds.

At the local pond or outdoor rink, the ice time is often free and a skater can stay until dark if he doesn't mind numb toes and chapped lips. Usually the rink needs to be cleared off and the boys shovel, sometimes for a couple of hours, piling the snow around the perimeter of the rinks. When no nets are available, shovels, boots and sticks take the place of goal posts. When the pick-up contests become too one-sided, the boys will play "shinny," a game in which one player has control of the puck and the others try to take it away from him.

The pond is a dreamer's world. When a boy has the puck he's Bobby Orr, Guy Lafleur or Rocket Richard, stickhandling his way through the defense and scoring the winning goal in front of a roaring crowd. For that moment, no matter how brief, he is in control. Problems like being a poor stickhandler are forgotten and when he loses the puck, the only thing in his mind is to regain it. In doing so his skills improve.

A baker's dozen of the players on the 1980 U.S. Olympic team grew up playing hockey in Minnesota. The state is the trendsetter of American hockey, a fact established by geography and climate, and

PHOTO COURTESY OF THE McCLANAHANS

Always ready for another game, Rob McClanahan logged a lot of ice time while growing up in North Oak, a suburb of Minneapolis.

are holidays thought of in hockey terms. Ask somebody, "What do you associate with Thanksgiving?" and most people will reply turkey, stuffing, cranberries or family. Ask the same question of Olympic forward Rob McClanahan and he will reply, "The pond back home will probably be frozen." As a boy growing up in St. Paul, McClanahan looked forward to the holiday because it was usually the first time of the new season that he could skate on the pond some 200 yards away from his parents' home. Winter after winter, McClanahan gathered his skates and walked down to the pond to play with the neighborhood kids.

Some 15 miles southwest of the McClanahan residence is the Twin Cities suburb of Bloomington and the house of John Mariucci, the godfather of Minnesota hockey. Born in 1916, Mariucci grew up in Eveleth, Minnesota, and attended the University of Minnesota at Minneapolis. He played end on Coach Bernie Bierman's football team and was a standout on the Gophers' undefeated hockey club. In 1940, Mariucci signed with the Chicago Black Hawks of the NHL and eventually was named captain of the team—a rare feat in a sport dominated by Canadians. Mariucci accepted the head coaching job at the University of Minnesota in 1952, and piloted the Gophers until 1966, when he joined the Minnesota North Stars, first as director of American player development and then as assistant general manager.

Mariucci spends a great deal of his time on the road, looking at prospective players and speaking with local hockey clubs. His home in Bloomington is near the Minneapolis/St. Paul International Airport because there is always another flight to catch, another hockey game to see in a distant city and never enough time. When he is home, though, Mariucci will often gaze out his front picture window at the pond across the street. Some enjoy the roar of the ocean or the wind in the mountain pines, but for Mariucci there is nothing like looking out on a sheet of ice and watching some boys play hockey. He will smile at their shouts and tumbles. Even though his belly now hangs over his belt and and his head is bald except for a fringe of grey, Mariucci is still a forceful personality. His opinion is taken as the gospel when the subject turns to hockey.

"So you want to talk about Minnesota hockey," he says in a low rasp: a voice than can quickly change from understanding to impatience and back again. "We'd better sit down. That's a big topic."

Mariucci is one of the founders and proponents of the "school system," an approach that combines education and hockey in the development of players. In Canada, still the foremost program for producing professional and, to a lesser extent, college, players, a youngster has to decide in his teens whether he is going to stay in school or pursue a professional career by signing with a junior team. There is no middle ground, and deciding to be a pro player is a gamble. If a teenager fails to make it in the pros he has little training or education to fall back on.

"Their system is archaic," Mariucci says. "They use a lot of individuals to attain an end. They have so many sacrificial lambs who go into the system and get neither an education nor hockey. The public looks upon those who have made it to the NHL and they think it's a great thing. But there are countless hundreds a year who end up with nothing."

In comparison, everyone who plays hockey in Minnesota ends up with something. Here, the first-rate teams are the high school and college clubs, and to stay on such teams a player must not only practice his slapshot, but hit the books. Michigan and upstate New York are among the areas of the United States that have copied the Canadian system, and the skills of the junior players are usually superior to the high-schoolers. The majority of the teams in these two states are all-star squads which select the best players for miles around. For example, Olympic defenseman Ken Morrow played on the Detroit Junior Red Wings, more than an hour's drive away from his home in Davison, Michigan. Most junior teams are private enterprise ventures and rarely are supported by the community. The clubs have difficulty drawing crowds because nobody in the immediate area recognizes the athletes and, as a result, many rinks and teams are in financial trouble.

The Minnesota high school teams, however, are made up of local players and have a large community following. The local arena in Roseau, Minnesota, home of the Olympic forward Neal Broten, seats approximately 2,500. Even though the town has about 2,000 residents, most high school contests are sold out.

Rinks are status symbols and revenue makers in Minnesota. Every town, no matter how small, wants a rink and if it has one already, it wants another. The 60 state invitational hockey tournaments make about $18 million annually, and it's estimated that the state has spent $180 million building Minnesota's 120-odd indoor rinks.

"When I talk to groups in other states, the first thing I warn them is 'Don't start up a junior program'," Mariucci says. "That's just so stupid. The high school and juniors fight themselves to the point where all the buildings go under. I tell them to look at our program. We have such an availability of facilities and such fans."

The final results of the Minnesota system, as advocated by Mariucci, have yet to be seen. Three junior leagues in Canada—the Quebec Major League, Ontario Major League and Western Hockey League —develop most of the athletes playing in the NHL. The best players from the youth leagues, some 720 total, are selected for these junior teams. The best of the juniors play in the NHL. The Minnesota system currently does not have the overall quality of the three Canadian leagues, but it does have a much larger base from which to build. About 150 high schools support varsity teams. With 20 players on each club, 3,000 potential NHLers play annually in Minnesota alone.

Each spring, the hockey season comes to an exciting close with the Minnesota State High School Hockey Tournament, held at the St. Paul Civic Center. Eight teams, the winners of rugged qualification rounds in all regions of the state, battle at St. Paul for the right to be called Minnesota's best. The three-day affair attracts more than 100,000 fans and such celebrities as Howard Cosell and Cheryl Tiegs have attended. "We're very much like basketball in Indiana," Mariucci says, "Each school has its following, and the frosting on the cake is to get to the tournament. The thing is sold out for months ahead of time, and the place is jammed for every game."

The tournament began in the early Forties. After seeing the large crowds attending high school games in the Twin Cities area, St. Paul athletic director Gene Aldrich proposed that the state have its own tourney. The first tournament needed financial assistance, but each succeeding championship has turned a profit, and the cumulative attendance has grown from 8,434 the first year to more than 100,000 in 1979.

Eveleth won the first high school state championship in 1945 and captured the title four times in the next six years. Two other northern schools, Roseau and International Falls, dominated the tournament in the Fifties and Sixties respectively. Roseau, which has appeared in the tournament a record 21 times, won back-to-back championships in 1958 and 1959, after finishing second in 1957. International Falls came home the winner three consecutive years, 1964 through 1966. Since 1967, no team has monopolized the tournament like those three schools.

PHOTO COURTESY OF THE VERCHOTAS   UNIVERSITY OF MINNESOTA PHOTO

Left: *In his senior year, Phil Verchota led Duluth High to the state tournament in St. Paul Minnesota.* Right: *Bill Baker moves in on the Notre Dame defense. The Gopher captain, Baker also received All-American honors while at the Univ. of Minnesota.*

Seven members of the U.S. Olympic team appeared in the state tournament while in high school. Neal Broten had the distinction of playing in the tourney as a freshman with Roseau High School. He returned to tournament action in 1977 and 1978, and was an all-state selection both years. Bill Baker, a four-year letterman at Grand Rapids, played on his school's tournament winner in 1975. Rob McClanahan of Mounds View and Steve Christoff of Richfield played in the 1976 tourney, and Christoff's Richfield team was the state runner-up. Phil Verchota led Duluth East to a surprise tournament berth in 1975, while goalie Steve Janaszak appeared with Hill-Murray High School. And in 1978, Roosevelt High of Minneapolis went to the state tournament with Mike Ramsey.

It's no coincidence that all seven ended up in Gopher uniforms. The University of Minnesota, known as "the U," usually has the pick of the tournament. Some 40 athletes a year receive hockey scholarships because of their performance in the tournament, and the most cherished prize for a player is to receive one of the six annual grants to play for the Gophers. "It's competitive, but playing for the 'the U' is a matter of state pride." said Bill Baker, one of the college's 21 hockey All-Americans.

The Gophers have not always enjoyed such a lofty reputation. In the early years, they were repeatedly trounced by teams that used more Canadians than Americans. Despite the losses, Minnesota stayed with state talent and, in 1953, the team received its first bid to the NCAA tournament. Even though the Gophers lost to Michigan, 7-3 in the finals, they demonstrated that Americans can compete against Canadians. The following year, Mariucci's third season as Gophers' coach, Minnesota again reached the finals only to lose in overtime to Rensselaer.

To help his program develop, Mariucci recruited a few Canadians to come south to play and to assist him in teaching the game. While most schools brought in Canadians who left after four years, Mariucci's imports stayed after their college eligibility ran out. Among his finds were Lou Nanne, Murray Williamson and Glen Sonmor. All three became major spokesmen for Minnesota hockey; Nanne was named general manager of the NHL's Minnesota North Stars, Williamson coached the 1968 and 1972 U.S. Olympic hockey teams and Sonmor worked his way up from Gophers' freshmen instructor to North Stars' coach.

"Some schools just went out for the best available player, and many of them were Canadians, which is fine," Mariucci says. "But at the end of their four years these Canadians invariably go back home. I went looking for the ones that I knew would never leave. I wanted the ones who would stay and make us better with their coaching."

The Gophers not only became better, they became champions. During Herb Brooks' six years as coach, the Gophers reached new heights, winning three NCAA titles, including the 1979 crown. That year's team had some familiar names on its roster like Broten, Baker, Christoff, Janaszak, McClanahan, Ramsey and Verchota. They were players who were winners in high school and college and, like their coach, were ready to take on the world at the Olympics.

Altogether, the Gophers have won seven league titles and have the best winning percentage of any school in the NCAA tournament play. Minnesota fans are easy to spot at most NCAA championships —they are often cheering the winning side, and they wear buttons which read 100% NATURAL INGREDIENTS, ACCEPT NO SUBSTITUTES, pointing out that their team is made of American skaters.

Though "the U" is Minnesota's showcase team, the rest of the state's hockey teams are impressive, too. In 1979, the year the Gophers won the NCAA crown, Bemidji State finished as the NCAA Division II runner-up, and the Minnesota Checkers came home with the national Open B Division women's title.

PHOTO COURTESY OF MRS. MARTHA JOHNSON

Mark Johnson at the age of thirteen on the neighborhood pond.

While Minnesota continues to grow on the youth, high school and college levels, the state faces its biggest hockey challenge with the Minnesota North Stars, labeled the "No Stars" for many years because of their inept play. The teams management brought in Lou Nanne as general manager and he began drafting more U.S. players in the late Seventies.

The addition of college players like Steve Christoff, Curt Giles and Mike Eaves helped transfer the clumsy "No Stars" into the fleet North Stars. Eaves was a star at the University of Wisconsin, and his coach was Bob Johnson, another Mariucci protegé and the father of Olympian Mark Johnson. "Bob was one of my boys," Mariucci says "and I feel that Mark is my grandson. He's second generation of what we started."

Fielding a team with eight Americans and two Swedes on its roster, Minnesota eliminated the Montreal Canadiens in the 1980 Stanley Cup quarterfinals. The defeat marked the first time since 1975 that the powerful Canadiens had lost a playoff series.

"Lou (Nanne) has stressed that he wanted a good skating team." says Glen Sonmor, North Stars' coach. "The people we have on this team are skaters, first and foremost. Lou's goal was to have a team that could skate and move the puck. We don't give them a lot of rules to follow out there. We just let them go."

In the Thirties basketball was Minnesota's winter pastime, but since then the state has become hockey mad. "Basketball's high-jumpers take a back seat to our rink rats now," Nanne says. "Hockey has become a state institution. It's the equivalent of Alabama football." And it's a fine beginning for an Olympic team.

CHAPTER 4

Fleet, Fast and Unlucky

Speed, it seems to me, provides
the one genuinely modern pleasure.

—Aldous Huxley

New Hampshire coach Charlie Holt looked baffled as he stood outside his team's locker room at the Detroit Olympia. "It was that kid," he said. "If we could have stopped him, we had a chance. But everytime we'd get close, there he'd go again." Holt's New Hampshire team had just lost to the Minnesota Golden Gophers in the semi-finals of the 1979 National Collegiate Athletic Association hockey championships.

That "kid," the player who undid New Hampshire's plans for a berth in the championship game against North Dakota, was Eric Strobel. The Minnesota forward scored three goals that evening for his fourth hat trick of the season. On each of his tallies, Strobel had stickhandled across center ice, faked toward the inside (and strength) of the New Hampshire defense and then quickly burst to the outside. His goals were a combination of speed and deception, the kind opposing players and coaches find frustrating to defend against.

The next evening, Minnesota played North Dakota in the NCAA finals. Minnesota won the contest, and the victory marked the third time in six years that the Gophers took home the first place trophy.

Forgotten in the cheering was how well North Dakota held the star of the semi-finals—Eric Strobel—in check. Turning in a sparkling performance in the preliminaries and then coming up empty in the finals became a habit Strobel has found difficult to shake. It has earned him the nickname of "Electric," because he is either outstanding or inconsequential on the ice. There are no in-betweens. During the Olympics, his act short-circuited and ended any hope of a quick entrance into the NHL. Unfortunately, he saved his poorest performance for the worst possible time and, as players like Mike Eruzione, Jim Craig and Rob McClanahan became house-hold names, during the Olympics, Strobel was on the fourth line for the final three games of the Games. Many parents of the Olympic players admit to watching him more than their sons in the pre-game warm-ups. The U.S. team was built on the theory that small, fast players

Eric Strobel outfakes the Princeton defense and moves in on goal.

could outperform big, slow players. When Ralph Cox, Les Auge and Jack Hughes were cut from the squad, the reason Brooks gave, time after time, was "lack of mobility." On the large rinks of international hockey, simple mistakes are disastrous, and a player who cannot make up for his errors by quickly skating back into the play becomes a liability.

For years, many experts have contended that Americans cannot skate with the rest of the world, specifically the Canadian players of the NHL. But one look at the play of U.S. team and athletes like Eric Strobel dispels such talk.

During the Pre-Olympic Tournament held in late December, Strobel was the star. When the Americans came out on the ice for the tournament's championship game against a Russian "B" team he received a loud ovation. The teams skated a few laps, warming up for a contest that marked the first time this U.S. team had played against a Russian squad. Strobel glided through a turn, bouncing on his skates and stretching from side to side. His blond hair, sticking out from underneath his helmet, blew back as he rounded the rink. He shot a puck at the net. It went past Craig, the starting goalie for the game, but hit the cross bar and bounced up into the crowd. Strobel laughed as some kids chased after the black disk. On one of his laps around the rink, he touched the inside of the left goalpost at one end of the rink with his stick. "I used to do it all the time in high school for luck," he said later.

On his first turn on the ice, Strobel took a pass from Mark Johnson and moved in on the Russian net. The goalie came out to make a pad save, and Strobel was checked and pinned against the boards to one side of the goal.

Midway through the second period, Strobel jumped over the boards on a line change and closed in on a Soviet player with the puck. Poking the disk loose with his stick, Strobel took control of the loose puck. Skating through center ice, he gathered speed and raced ahead of his teammates. At the Russian blue line, he was confronted by two defensemen. Taking one stride to the outside and then cutting back inside, Strobel darted in between the Soviet defensemen and challenged the goalie. Again the netminder made the save.

The ability to move in any direction at top speed is what makes Strobel better than most hockey players. Many just skate straight in on goal and, as a result, are easily guarded. Strobel, though, looks like a toy top let loose on a linoleum floor. By bringing his right leg quickly over his left, or his left over his right and leaning into a turn, he can move at top speed to either side. When he has possession of the puck, Strobel likes to move from one side of the rink to the other. This tactic confuses the competition, but occasionally bewilders his teammates as well. In one Olympic exhibition game, Strobel and winger Phil Verchota ran into each other at the opponents' blue line. The collision was mockingly called the best check of the night, and play had to be halted as both players lay on the ice and then slowly climbed to their feet.

Strobel's curious weaving patterns are an attempt to find unobstructed ice. Like a cowboy in search of wide open spaces, Strobel patrols the ice, looking for areas where he can outskate his opponents. Only 5'10", he avoids contact and rarely tries to check anyone. "It's surprising because in high school he played football and when he hit you, you were down." says his father, Art, a former professional hockey player. "But in hockey he doesn't go in for that. He likes skating and the finesse part of the game. He could take you out, but he'd just as soon go by you."

In the third period, Strobel ducked behind the Russian defense. Bill Baker fed him the puck and Strobel quickly shot it into the net. "That's the kind of play we used to do all the time at 'the U,' " Strobel said. "We're always looking for each other around the net."

The goal proved to be the winner, and the Americans defeated the Russians to win the tournament, a victory that was a clue of things to come for the U.S. team.

PHOTO COURTESY OF NANCY STROBEL

Eric Strobel was one of the first to make a name for himself in the Rochester, Minnesota, youth hockey program.

The child of a hockey household, Strobel began skating at the age of five. "There was a lot of hockey talk around our kitchen table when Eric was a boy," says his father. "It was just natural that he would listen and become excited about the game."

Begun at a young age, Strobel's love for skating hockey grew during grade and junior high school. "When I was little I used to go to public skating all the time," he said. "Every Friday night when I was little I would be at the Mayo Civic Aud—dancing and skating with all these girls. We listened to Monkee records back then.

"I always feel better after I skate. If I'm tired I try to go down to the rink and get in a work-out. Skating is a great release, my body feels better—it feels like everything is in tone and balanced."

Strobel was a stand-out on the baseball and football teams, but around Rochester, Minnesota, where he grew up, he is remembered as one of the first kids from the city youth program to receive a Gopher scholarship. Rochester, unlike Eveleth, Grand Rapids or St. Paul, is not a traditional hockey hotbed. The area is the only county in the state of Minnesota that does not have a natural lake within its boundaries. Strobel became a local hero when he was named to the all-state and All-American prep teams his junior year in high school. In 1976, his senior year, he was the state's leading prep scorer and upon graduation from Mayo High School, he went on to the University of Minnesota. Strobel led the Gopher freshmen in scoring his first year at "the U," inspiring coach Herb Brooks to call him "the best pure skater in the country."

The evening after the Pre-Olympic victory over the Soviet Union, Strobel sat in a Lake Placid bar, drinking beer and talking about his future. Selected in the eighth round of the 1978 amateur draft by the Buffalo Sabres, Strobel had made up his mind to turn pro even though he still had a year of college eligibility remaining. "I'll sign with Buffalo after the Olympics," he said. "Who knows? Maybe I'll be on teams that win the NCAA, a medal and the Stanley Cup in the same year. That would be something."

Strobel talked about the night that he, Mike Ramsey and Rob McClanahan, along with Buffalo coach Scotty Bowman and assistant coach Jim Roberts, had dinner at the home of Sabres' president Seymour H. Knox III. "The two coaches were really interested in our style of play, and they wanted to hear about it. I asked them if they thought the NHL would change to that kind of play. They said it would but that everyone right now is waiting for somebody else to be the first one to try it."

Strobel was excited about the possibility of becoming a Sabre, figuring Buffalo would be one of the initial teams to stress an international approach to hockey. Sometime after midnight, a stranger walked over to the table and placed a fresh beer in front of Strobel. "Good game, Eric," he said. "This is for you."

"I'm going to be watching this guy for sometime to come," the stranger announced. "I'm from Buffalo. You're joining a class organization—that club is strictly top shelf."

"I know," Strobel said, momentarily focusing on the empty beer bottles in front of him. "I'm happy to be going there."

Strobel and the Buffalo fan will have to wait a while before this gold medalist skates in the NHL, however. The Olympics were a replay of the second game of the NCAAs for the young forward. Again, he was held in check when everyone was watching. One play typified Strobel's dilemma. In the fifth game, Strobel skated through the West German defense and went in on goal, only to fall. Luckily, Neal Broten was nearby to put the puck in the net.

"I was finding toward the end I was losing confidence because I didn't know my role," he said after the Olympics. "I'd come into the locker room, and one night I'd be playing center and the next night I'd be playing wing. I was being switched around between lines. It got difficult. It kind of wore on me a little, but I figured I'm here and I might as well try my hardest—do my best. But I could see myself getting down."

As the goals became farther and farther apart, the Sabres' immediate interest waned, and Strobel began listening to several offers from Europe. Two German hockey teams, Cologne and Dusseldorf, had been trying to sign the fleet forward since his first visit to Europe in 1978. "They're talking a lot more money than I could make right now with Buffalo," Strobel says. "Although I want to see if I can make it here first, I do think about what it would be like over there."

Probably Strobel would be better off playing on the big rinks in Europe. His speed is something any NHL team would relish, but Strobel is considered too small and too timid to play in the pros. Displaying machismo by frequently slamming your opponent into the boards appeals to most coaches and some fans, and anyone who does not play that type of game is often considered a sissy. "Probably afraid to mess up his goldilocks." one NHL scout said of Strobel. Despite such scouting reports, the blond winger did give the pro game a try.

During the U.S. team's post-Olympic celebration in New York City, Strobel talked with Sabres' general manager, Scotty Bowman, and agreed to play the rest of the season on a game-by-game basis. He did not sign a long-term contract, however, because he wanted to keep his option open to play in Europe. Unlike Rob McClanahan and Mike Ramsey, the other Sabre draft picks on the Olympic team, Strobel played his first professional game in the minor leagues. He and Olympic teammate John Harrington were assigned to the Sabres' American Hockey League affiliate in Rochester, New York —about an hour's drive from Buffalo. The team is nicknamed the Americans, which fans often shorten to the Amerks.

"He should try Rochester and see how he likes it and then make up his mind whether he stays or goes to Europe," Art Strobel says. "Buffalo has a good team right now and I think Eric trying to make that club is a bit too much to expect. Of the three guys, (McClana-han, Ramsey and Strobel), my son has got to be low man on the totem pole."

A veteran of seven years in professional hockey, Mr. Strobel played for the NHL's New York Rangers during the 1943-44 season. Because he was a rookie and weighed only 140 pounds, Strobel spent most of his time on the bench. He never scored a goal in the NHL. "You had to earn your stripes back then," he says. "There were only a couple of guys allowed up to the big club each year, and once you made the team you were mostly a benchwarmer for a few years."

Near the end of his first season in the NHL, the elder Strobel injured his shoulder in a game against the Boston Bruins and never was the same player. The next year he failed to make the Rangers and for the next five seasons he played for the Hershey Bears of the AHL, trying to work his way back into the NHL. At 26, Mr. Strobel quit the game, moved to Rochester, Minnesota, and began working as an interior systems contractor, installing ceiling tile.

Twenty-nine years later, in another city called Rochester, Art Strobel's only son labored in the AHL minor leagues, waiting for his chance to play in the NHL.

The Amerks, like most minor league teams, are a group of former heroes and rising stars. Players like Dave Schultz and John Gould have been with NHL teams before and are now on the downward slope of their careers. They hope for one more trip to the big leagues, perhaps a share of playoff money to pay the mortgage on a split-level house in the suburbs that was purchased only a few years ago, when they were well-known names and the future looked so bright. Many spend the entire season living away from their families, who are miles away, in that home in the NHL city they left behind. Old-timers are usually composed. They score minor-league goals in a business-like manner, and when the puck enters the net they look back with disdain, probably wondering why they were not that easy in the big leagues.

The other group on any minor league team is the youngsters. Fresh from the junior or college ranks, they still play hockey because it is fun. They are enthusiastic, excitable and make mistakes. To-morrow is their time, and they know it. Some, if they're lucky and work hard, will play in the NHL, at least for a season or two. Near the end of the 1978-79 season, the Amerks welcomed two new youngsters—Eric Strobel and John Harrington.

In the pair's first home game, Rochester had a near sell-out. However, three days later the auditorium was only half-full as the Amerks prepared to take on the Syracuse Firebirds.

Rochester opened up a three-goal lead in the second period and had the game in hand early. Harrington had scored his first professional goal in the previous home contest and now the crowd began to cheer for Strobel to net one.

"Come on, Eric," yelled a young girl.

"Let's go, Strobel," bellowed a middle-aged man seated near the roof.

In the third period, Rochester defenseman Mike Boland lofted a long waist-high shot at the Syracuse goal. An instant later, he was checked against the boards by a Firebirds' winger. As the shot neared the net, Strobel changed the direction of the puck by deflecting it with his stick. Instead of being two-and-a-half feet off the ice, the puck was about three and the Syracuse goalie was unable to react in time. The puck went over his glove hand and into the upper left corner of the goal. The play only took seconds, but when it ended, Strobel had scored his first professional goal.

Later, outside the locker room, Strobel told a television reporter about the goal: "The shot was just coming in and I touched it with my stick. Nothing to it. I was in the right place, you know all that stuff. I wish they were all that easy."

At the far end of the corridor, about 20 kids waited for their favorite Amerks' player to come out of the locker room so they could get his autograph.

"Hey, mister, you got some blank pieces of paper?" one asked another waiting fan.

"Yeah," he replied. "Who are you waiting for?"

"Strobel," the boy said. Several others nodded their heads.

"Why him?"

"Cause he was the best guy out there," said one boy.

"Yeah," added another, "he skates pretty fast."

CHAPTER 5

The Iron Ranger

Much memory or memory of many things,
is called experience.

—Thomas Hobbes

A man is the reflection of his land. And for Olympic winger William Conrad "Buzz" Schneider, growing up on the Iron Range, a rocky string of mountains in northern Minnesota, taught him to be proud, patient and able to laugh at a world he was often struggling against.

It's a long road that leads to and from Babbitt, Minnesota, the small mining town where Schneider grew up. Nearly 250 miles from Minneapolis, it's a space in time which looks intimidating even on a map. Heading north out of the Twin Cities on interstate 35—better known to Bob Dylan fans as Highway 61—the land is flat and smooth. As the miles click by, the watertowers of each town become better guide-posts of how far you've gone and how far you still have to go than the mile markers. Like clockwork, the towers appear over the horizon—Mounds View, Wyoming, Pine City, Hinkley. Another 150 miles later, although the land around them had faded from fields of corn and grazing cows to forests of pine and birch, they still arise—Eveleth, Virginia and finally, Babbitt.

A town of some 3,500, Babbitt, like most settlements on the Iron Range, makes it living in the mines. The Range is populated by immigrants from Sweden, Finland, Italy and Yugoslavia, and most have been in America less than three generations. The traditional ways continue in Babbitt. Families are close-knit and broken English is still heard, with phrases like "Let's go out to the bar," becoming "Go out bar." The old world even gave Schneider his nickname. His aunt was the first one to call him "Buzz" which comes from the word "brother" in Yugoslavian.

The Reserve Mining Company is the big employer in Babbitt. Its open pit mine, 11 miles long and 115 feet deep, is in action 24 hours a day, seven days a week, every day of the year, except for short periods at Christmas and Labor Day.

Babbitt's tempo is controlled by the mine and when it's closed, life in the town below is interrupted. Five weeks after the U.S. hockey team's victory at Lake Placid, the mine was shut down as modifications were made to Reserve's plant on Lake Superior. For years environmentalists had argued that the company was polluting the waters of Superior with tailings from the factory. The battle went to the courts and when the environmentalists won, Babbitt received an unwelcomed vacation.

The parking lot outside the only bar within the town limits was crowded with cars. Inside, the tavern was just as packed, and the only empty tables were near the door.

"This is what you call cowboy time," Buzz Schneider explained. "You see, there's hardly any women in here. All these guys work in the mine and when it's closed down they don't know what to do with themselves, so a lot of them come here."

He rang the buzzer on the wall and soon a waitress appeared.

"Well, Buzzy, how are you?" she said. "What you want, a draft?"

"No, give me something bottled. Got any Pabst?"

"Bottled beer? He wins a gold medal and now he's drinking bottled beer," she joked.

The beers appeared on the table, and after taking a long swig, Schneider sat back in his chair and surveyed the crowd. The room was a collection of rain slickers, many of them with "Babbitt Steelworkers Credit Union" printed across the back. The Olympic hero seemed out of place in the smoky bar. He wore a USA jacket instead of a union slicker, and on his feet were clogs, not work boots. But Babbitt was still his home, and he was comfortable being back. Throughout the evening, husky voices from across the room shouted "Hey, Buzzy," and the hero would look up and salute another friend of his father's or his family's with a tip of his glass.

"This is where it all began for me," he said. "I've got some pictures at home of the parade they had for me after Lake Placid. It started three miles out of town and came in, and then they gave me some award over at the high school. I talked with the high school kids. Before the thing I had some pictures of me made up and signed them—must have been about 400, and I think I was handing them out all day."

After several Pabsts had piled up on the table, Schneider's father and the hero's high school coach, Ron Castellano, walked into the bar. A short man with a big smile, Castellano has the reputation of working his players hard on the ice and of being one of their best friends away from the rink. Former players, like Schneider, will have some beers and share a few jokes with him when they are back in town.

"Well look who's out looking for trouble," Schneider said.

"Nothing else to do," said his father. "I got some things around the house, but they can wait." The newcomers pulled up two chairs, and the waitress walked over to the table.

An hour later, the tabletop held a dozen empty bottles, cans or glasses, and Schneider was looking to move on.

"We're going out to the Foreign Service bar," he said. "You guys want to come along?"

"Why not? I'm already late to bed, what's a couple more hours going to do?" Castellano said. "Might as well come along. Don't get to see you much these days now that you're a star."

Located a couple miles out of town on route 21, the only major roadway running through Babbitt, the Foreign Service building houses the local chapters of the Veterans of Foreign Wars and the American Legion. Thus, the name Foreign Service, a title so strange that jackets from the organization are prized possessions throughout the Iron Range.

Inside, several patrons played pool, while everyone else sat at the bar, watching television and talking with the bartender. In the middle of the bar, there was a fishbowl with a shot glass submerged face up on the bottom. Pennies were scattered around the floor of the tank and none were in the glass.

"Can't remember anybody ever throwing one in there," Castellano said. "They've thrown them from the bar and put them in those up there," he said, gesturing at additional shot glasses which sat along the top of the liquor cabinet behind the bar. "They've put them in there all the time, but in that bowl that's different."

"The water seems to take them," Schneider said. "Throwing a penny from your stool into the bowl is easy, but I haven't seen anybody get one in the shot glass. Guess you get a couple of free drinks if you do it."

Pitching a penny from one's bar stool into the fish bowl, having the coin swirl and flip through the water and land in the shot glass—it's a feat that seems just as impossible as breaking into the NHL. Just ask Buzz Schneider.

After playing well in the 1976 Olympic Games at Innsbruck, Austria, where the U.S. team finished fourth, Schneider decided to turn pro. He was engaged to his girlfriend from Eveleth, and the time seemed right to begin making his fortune in the professional sports world of no-cut, six-figure contracts. The task proved to be easier said than done, however. For the next three years, Schneider went out for 11 different teams, on all levels of pro hockey. In a frustrating combination of bad luck and prejudice, Schneider found himself on team after team that was either overbooked with players who already had pro contracts or directed by general managers who thought Americans could not play the game. "I even heard that I

UNIVERSITY OF MINNESOTA PHOTO

Buzz Schneider, the only member of the 1980 Olympic Team who was on the 1976 club.

couldn't skate and that's ridiculous." he says. "I never thought of myself as an American hockey player. I thought that it didn't matter where you came from. If you were good enough, then you would play. But it didn't work that way."

Schneider's first pro try-out was with the Pittsburgh Penguins of the NHL. On the depth chart, the Iron Ranger was listed behind Vic Hatfield, Lowell McDonald and several other left wingers and was quickly sent down to Hershey of the American Hockey League.

Cut from that club, Schneider ended up with Oklahoma City of the Central League. He was there for three weeks, and played in two games. As at Pittsburgh and Hershey, the Oklahoma City roster was filled with players who already had a professional contract. There was no room for a player like Schneider, who was still negotiating a pact. When the axe fell at Oklahoma City, Schneider accepted an invitation to try out with Birmingham of the World Hockey Association. On the way to Birmingham, in the Dallas-Fort Worth airport, Schneider was paged to the phone by the Oklahoma City management. The team offered him a contract, but Schneider decided to turn it down. In retrospect, the refusal was a lucky move, because if Schneider had signed he would have been ineligible for Olympic play.

"I told them if things didn't work out, I'd come back, but by the time I did the offer no longer was there," Schneider says. "I went to Birmingham, and was there for a month and played in four games killing penalties. I was making good money—they were paying me a couple hundred a game and, after a while, $500 a week." But still Schneider could not wrangle himself a contract and was sent down to Hampton of the Southern League. He played there for two months until the league folded.

From Hampton it was on to Springfield and a 25-game try-out. "I thought I played real well, but like everywhere else I just felt that I never really got a chance." Schneider says. "Then John Mariucci called and asked if I was interested in playing in the world tournament [held in Katowice, Poland] and I said 'Sure, get me out of here.' "

The next season, 1977-78, began with Schneider in Hampton, this time in the American Hockey League. His stay was again short-lived and after a brief retirement, Schneider played the rest of the season for Milwaukee of the International Hockey League. The IHL is known for its rough play. In one game, Schneider was jumped by three opposing players when he was in the penalty box. Two players held him down and the third punched him on the back for several minutes. Schneider spent the next day in the hospital having his kidneys examined.

"What I remember the most about Milwaukee was the bus trips." he says. "It was at least a five-hour drive for every road trip because we were so far away from the rest of the teams in the league."

During the next summer, Schneider worked out, still trying to become the hockey player he believed he was. He ran up the hill to the mine, often wearing a 10-pound vest, touched the gate and ran back down to Babbitt. He lifted weights every other day and ran along Birch Lake. But when the 1978-79 season opened, the extra work did no immediate good. He started at the Chicago Black Hawks camp and was quickly sent down. "I was mad. I'd worked out all summer, and then I didn't make it."

Schneider ended up back at Milwaukee and got off to a fast start, scoring seven goals in his first five games. The club, though, was having trouble at defense, and Schneider, a player labeled as being a poor skater by some in the NHL, was shifted back to the blue line. "It was a good experience for me playing defense," he says. "But I thought I could play myself right out of that league if I had been playing up."

Midway through the year coach Herb Brooks called and asked Schneider not to sign a contract so he would be eligible for the 1980 Olympic team.

"If a good contract had come along I still would have taken it," Schneider adds. "But none did and I guess that was the way it was meant to work out."

The years in the minor leagues left Schneider experienced and eager to prove himself. He had played left wing, right wing, center, defense and killed penalties since his departure from the University of Minnestoa, and the Olympics gave him the opportunity to show off his new skills.

The morning after the late rendezvous at the Foreign Service bar, Schneider headed over to John F. Kennedy High School to borrow the keys to the hockey arena from Castellano. One of the first rinks in Minnesota to have plexiglass instead of chicken wire around the boards, the arena is well-insulated so ice can be made in the summer, which in this part of the country is about three months long. Schneider often skated at the rink, preparing for his next attempt at cracking the NHL. Even though the ice was not on today, the Olympic winger wanted to take a look around.

Walking through the halls of his old high school, on his way out to the rink, Schneider was recognized by many of the students who passed him. "This was a good place to go to school. Babbitt's a good place to grow up," he says. "Everyone who went out for a team made it, there were hardly any cuts."

Upon reaching the rink, Schneider opened the door, turned on the light switch and walked in. The ice surface is large. Many cities, let alone a town as small as Babbitt, would love to have a facility as expansive and as impressive as this one. In the near end of the rink, a batting cage was set up, netting draped around it.

While a student at JFK High, Schneider was a football, baseball and hockey star. In his senior year he not only received hockey scholarships, but a baseball offer from a college in Oklahoma. Eventually, he accepted a scholarship at the University of Minnesota because he wanted to play hockey and baseball. His freshman year, he did combine the two. In his sophomore year he was faced with a decision, however.

"They put together the national team (which played in Yugoslavia) and I was selected to go," Schneider says. "I wanted to play baseball, and maybe I liked baseball a little bit better than hockey, but when you're 18 years old and you have a chance to play in Europe, you're not going to turn it down, especially when you can play for your country."

Schneider played on the national team the next three springs and in the 1975 tournament he led the team in scoring with eight goals in

10 games, including a hat trick against the Russians. From then on baseball took a back seat to hockey in Schneider's life.

After being named to the 1980 U.S. Olympic club, Schneider was teamed up with Mark Pavelich and John Harrington, two other hockey players who learned their skills on the Iron Range. Harrington is from Virginia, Minnesota, about 35 miles to the west, and Pavelich hails from Eveleth, four miles south of Virginia.

The trio formed one of the U.S. team's most consistent lines and often had to sit out exhibition games, while coach Brooks tinkered with his other line combinations, trying to have them play as well as the Schneider-Pavelich-Harrington line, a threesome that became known as the Iron Rangers. Like all good lines, the trio had an uncanny knack of knowing where each other were on the ice at all times. The Iron Rangers were famous for their pinpoint passing, tenacious forechecking and the ability to score unexpectedly. Pavelich and Harrington had played together at the University of Minnesota at Duluth, and Schneider fit right in with the pair's style of play.

"I had played the whole year before in Duluth with Pav," Harrington says. "I knew how he played, so that was OK, and then Buzzy came in and he played the same basic kind of game—always moving, always going, looking for an opening."

"It got to the point where we just wouldn't look." Schneider adds. "We'd just throw the puck over there and somebody else on the line would be there. From growing up on the Range we played the same way. I don't know exactly what it was, but there was a chemistry there."

As the exhibition season progressed and the Iron Rangers became one of the Olympic team's top lines, Schneider found himself again having fun playing hockey. He was part of a team, and everyone was on equal footing in the fight to be one of the 20 players named to the Olympic team.

Buzz's wife, Gayle, selected photographs for yet another scrapbook on her husband. She had already completed four scrapbooks, two just on the Olympics, and now she was looking for "cute" pictures of Schneider as a child.

"Look at this one. Buzz in cowboy boots with a six-shooter," she said. "You were a real cowboy, weren't you?"

"Put that one back," Schneider said. "I don't want that in any scrapbook."

"No, it's too funny to leave out," Gayle said.

The weeks after the Olympics were an ordeal of sorting, packing, and storing things for Buzz and Gayle as they prepared to leave for Switzerland. Because of his exceptional play on the Olympic team, Schneider was offered a two-year contract with an "elite," or first division, professional team in Switzerland. The agreement includes the use of a car, an apartment, as well as more money than any NHL team was willing to offer him. With all their worldly goods stored in their parents' homes in Eveleth and Babbitt, there was plenty of work to do, but Schneider believes in the Iron Range philosophy of putting off until tomorrow, what was supposed to be done today.

"Gayle, I'm going for a drive," he said.

The streets of Babbitt are named after trees and in alphabetical order. Ash precedes Birch which is followed by Cypress. Out near the edge of town, where Elm Street is followed by Maple and Pine, is a sign which reads—"This town exists in spite of the following organizations: Sierra Club, Izaak Walton League, Friends of the Wilderness, Minnesota Public Interest Group and Minnesota Pollution Control Agency." The town could easily put up another sign alongside that one which would read—"Buzz Schneider has become a hockey hero, in spite of the NHL."

Yes, the man is a reflection of his land.

Buzz Schneider was a sharp shooter at early age.

PHOTO COURTESY OF THE SCHNEIDERS

CHAPTER 6

The Conehead Who Wouldn't Quit

The ones who live are the ones who struggle.
The ones whose soul and heart are filled with high purpose.
Yes, these are the living ones.

—Victor Hugo

The game was over and the squirt team from Virginia, Minnesota, had won. The club's coach was happy, pleased that his strategy of only playing his best players had resulted in a victory. Even though his tactics were criticized by some parents, the coach was proud of the win.

The Zamboni prepared to resurface the ice, and the two teams of nine and 10-year-olds made their way toward the locker rooms except for one player. John Harrington, one of those benched in order to win the game, watched his teammates leave and then hopped over the boards and began skating laps.

Around and around the rink he went. He carried his stick poised and ready, trying to copy the smooth-skating style of the other boys. The attempt, for now, was a clumsy parody. Head down, he dug his blades into the ice and leaned into the turns, trying to go as fast as he could without falling down, trying to prove to others that he was good enough to play.

A couple of laps later, Harrington got off the ice. The sweat on his face looked like tears.

Some players are born to greatness—able to smack a baseball out of the park and fly around a hockey rink at will. But others, like Olympic forward John Harrington, struggle every step of the way and become star players because of hard work and determination. From squirts to the U.S. Olympic hockey team, Harrington has rarely made a team without a struggle. And when he fell down or failed to make the club he always got back up and tried again.

One of Harrington's favorite sayings is "You play the way you practice" and his work-outs are more exhaustive than the games. He still keeps Zamboni drivers from their appointed rounds by gathering as many as 50 pucks and shooting them at the net after his teammates have left for the showers. In his shooting drills, Harrington selects one area of the net—upper left corner, lower right, upper right—and aims for it. A couple of misses in a row, and he will shake his head, muttering under his breath.

"Sometimes coach Brooks would leave practice early, and tell me to make sure that everyone gets off the ice," says Mike Eruzione, Olympic captain. "Harrington was one of those I had to beg to get off. I'd keep asking them, 'Please, fellows, get off the ice; I want to go home' and they'd just tell me to 'Buzz off.' "

Teammates at the University of Minnesota at Duluth, where Harrington played his college hockey, recall afternoons when John refused to talk to anyone in the locker room because he thought he had played badly in practice. Several even threatened to move to the other side of the locker room because of Harrington's behavior.

The sport which baffled Harrington the most as a kid was hockey. It took him many years of practice to master the game's skills, like shooting a slapshot or stickhandling past a defender. "In high school I enjoyed football more than hockey," he says. "I'm so emotional that I'm always getting mad at something, and hockey was frustrating to me because there were better players than me on our high school team. I'd always be trying to do something better than them."

Harrington's motto of "You play the way you practice" is an outgrowth of his family's slogan of "There's always room for improvement." All the Harringtons are persistent people. One of John's sisters insists that determination is a family trait, while his father, Charles, a locomotive engineer, contends that everyone in the family is stubborn and bull-headed.

The Harringtons keep an eye on each other, making sure everyone lives up to the family watchwords and philosophy. When John played hockey in high school, Mr. Harrington, a quick-witted Irishman, often told his son that he had played well, but reminded him that "There were times out there when I don't think you were working as hard as you could." Mr. Harrington often brought along his two brothers, also railroad workers, to back up his points about his son's play.

Later, when John was a teenager and talked about quitting, his father used reverse psychology and told him to go ahead and give up. "Well if Bah heard something like that he'd get that stubborn streak goin' in him, and he'd be right back at it," Mr. Harrington says.

John is called "Bah" (as in Humbug) by nearly everyone who knows him. His brother, who is 10 months older than John, constantly mispronounced the word "Baby" when the two were small children. He referred to John as "Bah," instead of "Baby," and the nickname stuck.

UNIVERSITY OF MINNESOTA-DULUTH PHOTO

John Harrington during post-Olympic Ceremony at Univ. of Minn.-Duluth.

"Bah" Harrington only began coming into his own as a hockey player when he made the Virginia High School team as a sophomore. He had failed to make the squad the previous year. However, this time he was one of eight players known as the "super sophs" who were named to the varsity team.

The super sophs were hard workers who never seemed to find enough ice time. They frequently stole into the arena at night. Somebody volunteered to play the organ and the players skated out of the locker room to the strains of the school fight song. It was a home game again, only without the crowd and the opposing team.

Dave Hendrickson, former high school hockey coach at Virginia, describes Harrington as a player who had to work on "his skating, agility and shooting" when he first joined the high school team.

"He had the ability, it just took a lot of hard work to bring it out," Hendrickson says. "He was always a little behind the rest of them, but he was gaining."

Hendrickson pushed Harrington hard in practice, and sometimes that bothered the high school coach. Several years after Harrington graduated from Virginia, Hendrickson asked him if he had been too demanding a coach in high school. Remembering his days on the squirt bench, Harrington laughed and said "No way."

In Harrington's senior year, Virginia was one of the best teams in the state. But the club lost to Grand Rapids High School, a team coached by Gus Hendrickson, Dave Hendrickson's brother, in the Iron Range District playoffs. Grand Rapids went on to win the state tournament, and Gus Hendrickson was named as the new coach at the University of Minnesota at Duluth. Playing in the state tournament gives high school teams and players a great deal of publicity and attention. However, annually, there are many other players, like Harrington, who are ignored because they never received statewide exposure. Without the publicity of appearing in the tournament, hardly any college teams were interested in Harrington. "After graduation I talked with quite a few coaches, telling them that when John caught up he was going to be some kind of player," says Dave Hendrickson. There were few listeners, and Harrington's grades, not his hockey ability, got him into the Air Force Academy. He went to Colorado Springs, immediately disliked the school and left. The joke around Virginia was that Harrington only stayed long enough to get a haircut.

"At the time I guess we were disappointed," Mr. Harrington recalls. "He had an opportunity to get an A-1 education, no matter what you say about the regimentation. But he had it in his head to play in the WCHA."

The Western Collegiate Hockey Association or WCHA, is considered by many to be the best college hockey league in the country, and for kids growing up in the Midwest, it's the only place to play. The opportunity to be called one of the best and able to play against the best was too tempting for Harrington. In late July, after leaving the academy, then trying out and failing to make the Colorado College team, he returned to northern Minnesota and went out for the University of Minnesota at Duluth team. Harrington received only a partial scholarship because all the athletic grants were already given out.

Like everything Harrington does, becoming a collegiate hockey star was an uphill task. His hustle and determination won him a place on the team as a freshman and he did receive a full grant the following year, but his performance was dismal. He scored only nine goals in his first season and five as a sophomore. He was benched during his second season, and did not make several road trips. In between his sophomore and junior years, Harrington worked out lifting weights and running more than five miles a day. He told his mother that he had to work very hard because he was unsure if he would be invited to join the team again in the fall.

At the beginning of his junior year, Harrington volunteered to play on the same line with sophomore center Mark Pavelich. A highly-touted player from the hockey hotbed of Eveleth, Minnesota, Pavelich had brilliant potential but had alienated most of his teammates, and few wanted to be on his line. Pavelich rarely played the traditional style of hockey; going up and down the ice in a predictable fashion. He frustrated everyone by skating erratically in and out of traffic and making his wingers look foolish by feeding them unexpected passes.

"Pavelich is a creator on ice, but his first season nobody could figure out what he was doing," UMD coach Gus Hendrickson says. "What he needed was a winger to finish off his creations."

Harrington was shifted from center, a position he had played since high school, to wing on Pavelich's line. The pair was a union of the hard worker and the natural athlete.

The new combination was successful, and the duo became UMD's most formidable offensive weapon. While some players try to stick-handle through the defense, Harrington and Pavelich used frequent, short passes to go around and through it. "I don't know how we do it," Harrington told a reporter his junior year, "we just say 'I'll see you down at the other end of the rink.' "

Pavelich finished the year with 14 goals and 30 assists for 44 points. Meanwhile, Harrington collected 22 goals, including five he scored when his team was playing a man short because of penalties. He had two shorthanded goals during the same penalty in a contest against Michigan and had a chance for a third, but a Wolverine defenseman tripped him before he was able to shoot. At the end of the season, Harrington was named UMD's most inspirational and most improved player. Ironically, he had also won his high school's most improved award as a junior.

Despite his success, Harrington was still a terror in practice, and occasionally chewed out his coach for being too easy on the team. "He was the kind of player that was very team-orientated and if somebody wasn't skating 100 percent, Bah would tell them that," says Gus Hendrickson. "He could not take someone who didn't hustle."

Nobody caused Harrington more frustration in practice than his own linemate, Mark Pavelich, who considered workouts a waste of time, and saved himself for the games.

"We were the first line and there were days when the fourth line, which works the hardest of anybody anyway, would be taking us apart, going around us for easy goals," Harrington says. "And Pav would be taking it easy. I'd keep saying to him, 'Come on, will you just try?' I just wanted to be better than everybody that was across from me."

The next season, the pair received national attention as they led UMD to the third place in the WCHA, behind North Dakota and Minnesota, the school's best finish ever. Pavelich finished third in the WCHA scoring race and might have won it from Colorado College's Dave Delich if he had not been injured for four games.

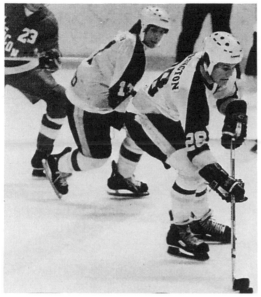

Mark Pavelich

UNIVERSITY OF MINNESOTA-DULUTH PHOTO
John Harrington (28) and Mark Pavelich cross the
Wisconsin blue line.

Harrington ended the year tied for fourth with future Olympic teammates Steve Christoff and Neal Broten at 59 points.

Upon graduation from UMD, Harrington wanted to play in Europe. However, Steve Sertich encouraged him to go out for the 1980 Olympic team. "Steve said 'Someday you'll kick yourself in the butt for never trying out for the Olympic team,' so I decided to give it a shot," Harrington says.

Harrington left for Colorado Springs and worked out with Sertich, co-captain of the 1976 Olympic team, for six weeks before the Olympic tryouts in mid-July, 1979. Harrington pushed himself seven hours a day—running, skating, lifting weights and taking ballet lessons.

The efforts succeeded. Harrington, along with Pavelich, were among the 26 athletes chosen to the Olympic hockey squad. In the first two months of the six-month, 61-game, schedule, the pair saw little action, and Harrington felt they were being ignored by coach Brooks. "In practice we'd be taking turns on the power play and when it was our turn he'd skate down to the other end of the rink and do something else," Harrington recalls. "In the locker room one day after a couple of hours of this I looked at Pav, and he said, 'We're just the Coneheads around here.' "

Brooks, though, was impressed by the UMD duo and as the exhibition season progressed he gave them more ice time. With the addition of Buzz Schneider at left wing, the line was labeled the Iron Rangers, instead of the Coneheads.

Off the ice, Harrington, with assistance from Dave Silk and Mike Eruzione, kept track of the slogans Brooks repeated over and over until they became team clichés. The best "Brooksisms" were logged in a spiral notebook and by the end of the exhibition season there were more than 16 pages of entries.

Harrington's favorite was, "He's got a nickel brain and a million-dollar pair of legs."

"Brooks told me that one a lot," he says.

After the U.S. won the gold medal at Lake Placid, Harrington described the event at the post-game press conference in a glowing string of Brooksisms.

"Well, we were damned if we did and damned if we didn't. We looked like a bunch of monkeys screwing a football out there for a while but we rebounded, used our youth, took our hard hats and lunch pails to work, went right up to the tiger, spat in his eye and punched him in the face. It was a pretty good example of why we won the game and, in nutshell, for lack of a better phrase, that about wraps it up."

One of the prized possessions in the Harrington household is an eight-millimeter film of the first time John went skating at the age of five. Taken at Kenny Park in Minneapolis, the film is brought out at family gatherings and it shows John stepping onto the ice for the first time, trying to skate, and, of course, falling down.

"In our house when that comes on everyone's got the whole choreography down," Harrington says. "Everyone does the play-by-play, knowing exactly when I'm going to fall."

"Anyone looking at that film would be in disbelief that a hockey player could develop from that," says his mother.

The film is short and the family will often replay it, laughing as if they are watching a Charlie Chaplin or Buster Keaton movie. They are not only amused by the brief picture show, but are also proud of it. The film ends with Harrington sprawled on the ice, struggling to stand up.

CHAPTER 7

The Kid from Bunker Hill

And this brought forth a dream and soon enough,
This dream itself had all my thought and love.

—William Butler Yeats

Across the river from downtown Boston, east of the university world of Harvard and MIT, is Charlestown, Massachusetts. Giving up much of its shoreline to the United States Naval Yard, bordered to the north by the Mystic River and criss-crossed by two expressways, this neighborhood has little of Boston's sophistication or Cambridge's tranquility. The two-story buildings are packed tightly together. Children play in the streets, rarely stopping their games when cars drive up the narrow avenues. The kids here have to be tough, for they are major players in a daily drama in which competition, compassion and violence exist in a fragile and often broken truce.

To outsiders, Charlestown is a world to be read about in newspapers. The neighborhood has been in the frontlines of busing, the rise in student drug use and the increased crime rate. Today's murder or misunderstanding is tomorrow's headlines. But under this film of bad publicity is an Irish-Catholic neighborhood that still believes in hard work, sacrifice and dreams.

A couple of blocks from the town's only string of stores is Eden Park. The chain-link fence around the tennis courts has been pushed outward from the inside, as if something or somebody was struggling to be free. The fence's ruptured appearance is due to the repeated pounding of a street hockey ball, an orange sphere which is weighted so it will not bounce.

There are no pick-up games at Eden Park. Street hockey leagues are formed and the townies line up two and three rows deep to watch the contests. Stickhandling around the posts intended to hold up tennis nets, the kids shoot low, hard drives at the goal—the kinds of shots that eventually bend fences.

Up the hill from the park is the Bunker Hill monument. A towering, granite statue, resembling the monolith in Arthur C. Clarke's *2001, A Space Odyssey*, the memorial commemorates the 1775 battle in which British soldiers were twice beaten back by an American militia. The colonial upstarts were forced to retreat on the third attack after running out of ammunition, but not before killing almost half the British force.

The monument casts a long shadow on Charlestown. It's a reminder of the impossible feats an individual can accomplish if he believes and works. A half-block from Bunker Hill is the home of the O'Callahan family.

The second of three children, Jack O'Callahan began organized hockey at the age of eight when Father Robert Smith, a priest at a local church, recruited him for his Sunday night team. Within two years, O'Callahan was playing Saturday afternoons and evenings, as well as Sunday nights. Other nights of the week he and his friends would sneak into Boston Garden, only a 10-minute walk away, to watch the NHL Bruins. After attending St. Catherine's Grammar School, O'Callahan was accepted into Boston Latin High School and was elected the most valuable player on the hockey team in his junior and senior years. Boston Latin is one of the best high schools in Boston, and the oldest such educational institution in the U.S. It has high standards which all students, including athletes, must maintain. O'Callahan not only kept his marks above average, but received all-scholastic honors. The combination of good grades and his hockey ability meant O'Callahan was heavily recruited by Harvard, Brown, and Boston University during his senior year. The choice soon came down to Harvard or BU, and even though his father wanted him to go to Harvard, O'Callahan thought he would be unable to excel in both the classroom and hockey rink at Harvard and picked BU.

Playing defense for the Terriers, O'Callahan had an impressive college career. He won the team's most valuable player award his junior and senior years, was the team captain and an All-American. In the classroom he majored in American history, and was BU's top student-athlete in 1978. During college, O'Callahan took tours of Boston, learning architectural styles and the city's history. Driving with him through the streets of Boston is a rapid-fire bicentennial minute. He moves from one side of the car to the other, gesturing at buildings, telling when they were built, and pointing out the subtle differences which make one house a landmark and another a contemporary copy cat.

In between his junior and senior years at BU, O'Callahan played for the U.S. National team in Prague, Czechoslovakia, and in 1979, he was on the American team which played in Moscow. Even though he was selected in the 1977 amateur draft by the Chicago

BOSTON UNIVERSITY PHOTO

Jack O'Callahan in college action.

Black Hawks, professional hockey would have to wait. The possibility of playing for his country on the Olympic team kept O'Callahan from signing an NHL contract. In July 1979, the former BU defenseman was named to the U.S. Olympic team.

During the exhibition season, O'Callahan's previous international experience and inspired play made him a standout at defense, the team's weakest position. He led the American defensemen in points before twisting his knee in a game against Birmingham of the Central Hockey League. O'Callahan sat out two weeks of the exhibition schedule in mid-November, and the leg recovered. However, in the final exhibition game, at Madison Square Garden against the Russians, O'Callahan again twisted the knee and it was considered improbable that he would play at Lake Placid.

The Russian game was a Saturday afternoon contest, and the U.S. team's first Olympic contest was that Tuesday evening against Sweden. Each club's final roster, only 20 players, had to be turned into the Olympic officials by noon Monday. After that deadline, no new players could be added or deleted from the line-up.

From late Saturday afternoon until Monday morning, O'Callahan wondered if coach Herb Brooks would name him to the team. "I had more points, more ice time than any other defenseman. I said to myself, 'He can't throw me off this team. I mean too much to it.' " O'Callahan recalls. "Then again if I can't play, he's got to. There were two parts of me, the rational part and the emotional part arguing inside my head."

Saturday evening the team arrived at the Olympic Village, and O'Callahan went to bed, his leg propped up with a pillow and an ice bag on top of his knee to keep the swelling down. He tried to sleep, but spent the night staring at the ceiling. At six the next morning, he limped over to the medical tent and was examined by Dr. John Steadman, physician for the U.S. ski team and the one responsible for putting skier Phil Mahre's ankle back together. The night of no sleep and anxiety had caused O'Callahan's hamstrings and muscle groups surrounding the knee to tighten. The damaged area was stiff and inflexible when Steadman examined it, and he concluded that most of the ligaments were torn and the defenseman would be in a cast for the next eight weeks. O'Callahan went to bed and cried himself to sleep. His Olympic dream seemed to be over.

"I didn't know we were going to win a gold medal," he says. "I didn't even care. I just wanted to be in the Olympics. That's why I stayed out of pro hockey. That's what I've been thinking about for years and here it is, a few days before the Olympics, and I'm hurt."

At 11 A.M., O'Callahan woke up and went to the phone trailer to call his parents. While his mother cried, O'Callahan and his father discussed whether the family should still come up to Lake Placid. It was eventually decided that the family would drive up if O'Callahan was named to the team. After he hung up, O'Callahan sat alone in the trailer. Unexpectedly, Dave Silk, a former BU player, walked into the trailer. A casual "How are you doing?" was answered with only a shake of the head from the usually vocal O'Callahan.

"What's with you?" Silk asked.

"I'm going to be cut," O'Callahan said, and the pair broke into tears.

Sunday afternoon, less than 24 hours before the final U.S. roster had to be submitted, O'Callahan saw two more doctors. The additional examinations indicated that even though O'Callahan did have some torn ligaments, he still had enough strength in the leg to play in the Olympics.

"At this point I hated Steadman," O'Callahan says, "because he told me it was torn. But when he examined me this time he found it was mostly a bad sprain. He said 'If you want to play you've got a long road ahead and I don't think you'll be ready. But if you want to work maybe five times as hard as anyone else, then you'll be able to play in three or four games.' "

Monday morning, the U.S. team and O'Callahan were in the locker room, while American coaches and doctors debated in the corridor outside about what to do with the injured defenseman. It was only hours before the roster deadline, and the U.S. team was faced with an agonizing decision. If O'Callahan was named to the team and could not play and then additional Americans were injured, the club would be hardpressed, especially on defense. Forward Dave Christian was already playing defense and there was one reserve left, Bob Suter, to fill in at the blue line. Still, many members of the team thought O'Callahan deserved a chance to come back.

Coach Brooks entered the locker room, and announced, "Jack, we've had a long talk and we don't know if you're going to be able to play, but we're going to stick with you." The coach and O'Callahan embraced as the team cheered.

"Looking back on it, that was just about the best thing Herb could have done," says team captain Mike Eruzione. "The emotion in that locker room was a great way to start off the Olympics."

While the team prepared for its first game against Sweden, O'Callahan teamed up with Bruce Kola, a trainer from Colorado College, and began rehabilitating his knee. With a tape recorder and cassettes of popular music to help him forget the pain, O'Callahan did isometric exercises, squat thrusts and one-leg sit-ups, lifted weights and rode a stationary bicycle. After each work-out he went to the U.S. medical tent to have the leg iced, and to the Olympic hospital for whirlpool treatments.

"I was doing that three times a day, "O'Callahan said. "I'd get up at seven in the morning, work out, then do it at three in the afternoon and again at 10 at night. In the meantime, I was seeing doctors every day."

O'Callahan's efforts soon became the talk of the medical world at the Olympics. When he visited the ski jump to take pictures, the residing physician at the site asked if he could see the damaged knee. "It seemed every time I went into the medical tent, or anywhere, I was taking off my clothes so some other doctor could bend it and make his own diagnosis and then they would compare diagnoses."

The day after the Sweden game, O'Callahan was back on skates and for Thursday's game against the Czechs he was in uniform, although he was still too weak to play. Getting ready for games and practices was a time-consuming procedure as moleskin and adhesive cloth, stronger than normal tape, was wrapped around O'Callahan's leg from hip to foot. The toe was pointed to the inside to keep the ligaments from stretching, so when O'Callahan stood up it looked like his right leg was pigeon-toed. The taping made skating more difficult, and there was still danger every time he took the ice. "All the tape in the world couldn't have saved him if he had gotten hit again like he did in the Russian game [at Madison Square Garden]," says trainer Bruce Kola. "I guess it's safe to say that he would have torn the ligament and that would probably require surgery. But the doctors outlined the risk to Jack, and he knew what he was doing."

"It is unusual to have an athlete take the risk he did coming back so quickly from the injury," says Dr. Steadman. "But for Jack, the Olympics were a once-in-a-lifetime event and he knew the stakes. He knew what he had to lose and gain.

"I think Jack's case should not make every kid think he ought to go back out and start playing after an injury," Steadman says. "It should be emphasized that what Jack did was take a chance on further injury and because he came back so soon he had to take the summer off before joining the NHL."

In Friday's practice before the Norway game O'Callahan's skate hit a rut and he fell, again retwisting the knee. The doctors and Brooks kept him out of uniform for the game, and it looked like O'Callahan would indeed spend his Olympics on crutches in the stands. After several work-outs with the weights and on the stationary bicycle, though, O'Callahan was back in uniform. In the contest against Romania, nine days after he had injured the knee in Madison Square Garden, O'Callahan was on the ice during the power play and taking an occasional turn at defense. Even though he was now playing, O'Callahan continued to work out three times daily until the end of the Olympics.

When the U.S. team took the gold medal with its victory against Finland, Jack O'Callahan showed up at the post-game press conference, bottle of beer in hand. He stood up on top of the table and fielded questions from the press.

Jack O'Callahan was a townie from way back.

"The Americans won at Bunker Hill!" he shouted, "and Americans won at Lake Placid!"

"Where did you learn your history?" a reporter asked. "The Americans didn't win at Bunker Hill."

"I don't want to hear that," O'Callahan replied. "Why do you think there's a monument there?"

In Charlestown, after the Games, O'Callahan was the neighborhood's new hero. On a wall of a brick building down the street from Eden Park, slightly obstructed by a blue van with two flat tires, were the words, "Jack O' USA hockey" and the outline of a shamrock.

"That's what they're writing on the walls now instead of nigger or bastard," O'Callahan says. "It's kind of weird, isn't it?"

Proud to call himself a townie, O'Callahan contends that growing up in Charlestown was a major reason he became a gold medalist. "There's a fever on the streets, a kind of emotion here," he says. "It grips you and makes you go. I put that power into sports."

Charlestown has literally left its mark on O'Callahan. Three scars —one running down his left cheek and two near the ear—are the results of a bar room scuffle. One night the defenseman and a couple of friends were having a few beers at a local pub when a kid attacked O'Callahan from behind and scraped a broken bottle across his face.

Down a winding street in back of the new Charlestown high school is a parking lot and, next to it, a small park. The trees, planted only a few years ago and still held upright by wire and splints, are dying. The strawlike grass competes with the weeds and litter for sunlight. O'Callahan was a counselor for one of the summer work crews which cleaned up the parks around Charlestown. Walking around his old neighborhood, O'Callahan often sees boys he used to work with on those summer work crews. One such kid was Johnny Fitzpatrick.

"It happened right over there," O'Callahan says, pointing across the small inlet which separated the parking lot from the projects. "Johnny was walking through there when these guys, high on angel dust or something, started chasing him. One of them with a knife caught up to him and cut his heart out. That kid would have been a great athlete—a good person, but now . . .

"There are two choices for every kid here—you can stand on the corner and smoke and become a derelict or you can play sports on some team. When I was a kid, the peer pressure was to be on a team and stay in school because that's what your friends were doing. Now the peer pressure is the other way. It's for saying 'screw this' and deciding not to do anything. And the chance a lot of kids have, the only way to be something better, is thrown away.

"I don't think my gold medal will help things like that. Two or three months from now the effect will have worn off, and the kids will be back on the corners."

The next evening a motorcade, with O'Callahan in the lead car, traveled the streets of Charlestown, bound for a $6-a-plate dinner honoring the Olympic defenseman at the Bunker Hill Knights of Columbus meeting hall. As the motorcade wove its way through town, a young boy ran alongside O'Callahan's car, his hand resting on the door. In the hall, there were more people than seats, and additional folding chairs and tables were set up against the far wall. "There's people here I haven't seen in 20 years," said O'Callahan's father. A half-hour later, the motorcade pulled up in front of the hall.

The head table at the banquet read like a meeting of the clans, with names like Flynn, Donovan, O'Neil and Flannagan. Five Olympic rings hung from the ceiling, and a musical group (coincidentally named the O'Callahans) performed Irish jigs and ballads. The party honoring the gold medalist went on into the night. Dinner was forgotten, and beer and drinks became the main course of the evening. Nearly every speaker had a gift for O'Callahan—license plates with his Olympic number 17 on them, plaques, silver serving trays and spending money. When the last speaker had finished, the O'Callahan family was introduced and watching them, Jack's eyes became misty and he wiped away the tears with his napkin.

Then it was the moment everyone had waited for—O'Callahan's speech. The lights were dimmed, and O'Callahan nervously looked around the room as he got up to the podium. He smiled and then talked about what it was like at the Olympics, and then, he spoke about being a townie.

"I've been everywhere this year, but I still couldn't wait until I was back home in Charlestown with you," he said. "Life is tough, but I remember parents helping their kids, trying to give them something better. I guess that is what I think about when I think about Charlestown. Parents helping their kids get by, giving them something."

In closing, O'Callahan added: "People may talk about me and what I did, but I'll tell you who is the real hero tonight. That kid who ran next to my car during that parade. Is he here?"

A boy, 10 or 11 years old, was pushed up to the head table. He looked at the audience and then at O'Callahan with saucer-like eyes as the Olympic defenseman took his gold medal and hung it around the boy's neck.

"I don't believe this," the boy said, looking at the medal as the crowd cheered. For at least one young boy, the Charlestown dream was as good as gold.

CHAPTER 8

Shelter from the Storm

You Can't Go Home Again

—Thomas Wolfe

Mike Eruzione, captain of the U.S. Olympic hockey team, disagrees with Thomas Wolfe's wisdom. He argues—politely, logically and with humor—that a person can always go back home. He, for one, does it all the time. While many of his Olympic teammates donned NHL jerseys after Lake Placid, Eruzione took his bright smile, his belief in America's inner greatness and hit the road. But no matter how far he roams, he contends, like Dorothy in *The Wizard of Oz*, that "there's no place like home." Winthrop, Massachusetts, is Eruzione's version of Kansas; a place where the famous Olympian knows there is a plate of lasagna and a household of laughter and relatives waiting for him.

Stepping off the air shuttle at Boston's Logan Airport, Eruzione smiles. At least for a few hours, until tomorrow morning, he is back home. The next morning he would fly to New York, and the next day on to Washington. He would return home three days after arriving in Washington and then leave again for Florida. He would be back home again four days later. When Eruzione explains his hectic schedule, the day he comes back home to Winthrop is emphasized as much as his next departure and destination.

Like the other Boston boys—Jack O'Callahan, Dave Silk and Jim Craig—Eruzione is nearly as popular in New England as the Pope or a Kennedy. People love to hear him talk about the old-fashioned principles like loyalty to one's country, pride in one's self and love for one's family that he insists were the reasons for the U.S. hockey victory at Lake Placid. Forget pucks, sticks and shots on goal. The gold medal win was more cosmic than that and, in Eruzione's opinion, the victory was typically American.

"I can't remember another country pulling off something like that," he says. "We showed that this country is still great, and if everyone works hard at what they do best, we'll do OK. We proved that with a little hard work, loyalty, pride and love, too—because we loved each other—a person can be successful."

BOSTON UNIVERSITY PHOTO

Mike Eruzione won the ECAC award for the best defensive forward four years in a row.

Eruzione was the captain of unknowns and unheraldeds, so it was only fitting that he scored the most memorable goal—the winner against the Russians. Everywhere he goes now, people shake his hand, ask for his autograph and thank him for defeating the Soviets. He is also remembered as the player who decided not to go into professional hockey, even though five NHL clubs wanted to sign him after Lake Placid.

"Being captain of the Olympic hockey team is a fine way for me to get out of the game I love," he explains. "I've reached the highest goal for me. The Stanley Cup is the big thing in the NHL and I don't think a Stanley Cup can equal a gold medal.

"I knew for me to play in the NHL I would have to bust my butt each time on the ice. I don't think I could have played 80 games a year like I played the Russian game. So why cheat them and why cheat myself? I don't want to be remembered as a struggling young hockey player. I want to be remembered as the captain of the team that won the gold."

Such statements have made Eruzione a sought-after celebrity and a media hero. He was the guest speaker at a series of IBM symposiums, and reportedly received $10,000 a day for giving a five-minute pep talk to groups of salespeople. He was a guest star on "The Mike Douglas Show" and the "Hollywood Squares." There were other appearances at golf tournaments, telethons, and talk about filming a movie of his life. Within six weeks of stepping off the victory platform with his gold medal, Eruzione was booked until next Christmas. Despite the newfound fame and attention, Eruzione keeps his life in perspective. "I think it's funny for a guy from Winthrop, Mass., to go from complete obscurity to being a national hero and speaking all over the United States.

"My family played an important role in the way I've handled everything." he adds. "I think the only reason I've kept everything under control is that I know what it's like to grow up in a big house."

When Eruzione talks about his travels, he often describes events and people he meets in terms of how well his family would have liked them. After meeting Danny Thomas, Eruzione told his father: "He was a real good guy and, you know something? He doesn't even drink the coffee he sells on TV."

A fifteen-minute drive from Logan Airport is one of the smallest communities in the state, a quiet, green neighborhood of parks and two-story houses called Winthrop. The town is located on a thin peninsula that forms the northern jaw of Boston Harbor. From the top floor of some houses in the town, both the Atlantic Ocean and Boston can be seen.

Winthrop was founded in the 1630s by John Winthrop, after a previous settlement failed in Charlestown. The Winthrops were a family of politicians. John was a seven-time governor of the Massachusetts Bay Colony, and his son and grandson were governors of Connecticut. But in the Town of Winthrop, the most endeared family member was Deane Winthrop, who stayed home and out of politics. He lived in a house on Crystal Cove, some nine blocks away from the Eruzione home. Deane Winthrop became well known for his novel method of signaling the arrival of a ship. When a boat appeared on the horizion he hoisted a bush to the top of a tall pole, informing the dockworkers in Boston that a vessel was approaching the harbor.

Around Boston, the Town of Winthrop is known as a good place to raise a family. Because the community is located outside the city limits, it was not involved in the busing riots of the mid-Seventies. Winthrop is the kind of town that used to exist before the American family disbanded and moved to a split level in the suburbs or a downtown apartment. Old men sit in the town square, a small park at the crossroads of the town, that is as picturesque as a Norman Rockwell painting and as innocent as the Beatles' song "Penny Lane." It's only a half block up the street from Winthrop's only McDonald's Restaurant and shopping mall. The town hall, fire department building, public library and monuments honoring the war dead, from the Spanish-American to Vietnam Wars, are the major landmarks in the square.

The Eruzione residence is on Bowdoin Street, a short walk away. A large green house with dark trim, the house has three floors and members of the Eruzione clan on every level. Mike Eruzione grew up on the second floor, and it was common for him to go up to the third floor or down to the first and eat with his aunts and uncles, nieces and nephews if he did not like what was on the table at his home. The front door of the Eruzione home is rarely locked, and the footsteps of visitors echo up the wooden staircase in resounding "clunks."

Some 17 family members live under this roof, but no one is really sure of the exact total because there are usually additional relatives staying over. Inside, the atmosphere is uproarious and noisy. The house plays host to gatherings of 200 high schoolers, sing-alongs until 2 A.M. and family reunions on every Labor Day and Fourth of July. Once Mike brought home six Olympic teammates—Bill Baker, Mark Johnson, Eric Strobel, John Harrington, Buzz Schneider and Dave Christian—for dinner. All were amazed by the Eruziones and their home.

"They just slid some chairs over and squeezed us in around the table," Schneider says.

"I was introduced to so many people in such a short period of time, that I lost track of who I was talking to." Harrington says. "We're packed around that table and every other minute somebody would walk in and Mike would say, 'This is my cousin' or 'my sister's husband' or 'their kid.' I just couldn't keep up with all of them."

The first person to greet a visitor to the second floor is Mike's mother, Helen Eruzione. A short, plump woman, Mrs. Eruzione was famous in Winthrop before her son came home with a gold medal. Her cooking, especially her lasagna and ravioli, draws rave reviews. "She's a great person and a great cook," says Peter Burke, a guidance counselor at Winthrop High School. "When you get invited to the Eruziones for dinner, all other appointments are put aside."

Mrs. Eruzione works during the day as a matron at the high school, supervising the cafeteria and the girls' lavatory. Late in the afternoons, she returns home and begins making dinner: a meal that sometimes serves as many as 15 people. As she works in the kitchen, cars park outside on Bowdoin Street. The Eruziones are coming home, and soon the family living room will be as crowded as the street out front.

It's Friday, one of the rare evenings that Eugene Eruzione does not have to work as a waiter at Santarpio's, a pizza place in East Boston. For much of his life, Mr. Eruzione has worked two jobs to support his family. During the day he works at the Deer Island sewage treatment plant, and most evenings he is at Santarpio's. Mike's first pair of hockey skates, in fact, were purchased with tip money from Mr. Eruzione's second job. But tonight, instead of waiting on tables, Mr. Eruzione sits on the sofa with several of his daughters and watches his grandson, Anthony, crawl across the floor.

The television is on and the screen fills with the latest from Iran, Afghanistan and the White House, but nobody pays much attention. The group only quiets when a commercial comes on or when there is an update on the weekend weather report. Sitting in her chair by the door, Mrs. Eruzione looks over her family.

"I've always told my children to get along with everybody," she says. "There's something you can learn from everyone if you look for it and pay attention. But I also told them that when you decide to do something, set a goal and don't worry about everybody else. When you decide you want something, make sure you keep working."

When the conversation turns to Mike, their gold medalist son, the Eruziones are justifiably proud. They have been his loyal supporters since grade school, and all of them have their own favorite story about him.

"He was the spark and the motivator of his high school team," Mr. Eruzione says. "In one game he got cut above the eye and he wouldn't go off and get stitched up. He only had a band-aid on it and it kept bleeding. His coach [Paul O'Brien] was behind the bench, and he turned around and looked for me up in the stands. When he saw me, he told me to get him out of there."

His sister Nancy remembers her brother as a hero in high school. "Michael always gave us a thrill," she says. "He was always good for the big goal, the winning home run or throwing the touchdown pass. Then he went on to BU and he kept doing that."

"Everyone knows about his goal against the Russians," Mr. Eruzione says. "But what people don't know is he's been doing it that way for years."

"He's there in the critical situation," adds Nancy.

In his imagination, Eruzione practiced those critical situations over and over again while playing in his side yard, a field he nick-named "Three Cousins Stadium." The empty lot was his playground as a kid, and now it is used by cousins and nephews. A number of sports—stickball, football, basketball and street hockey—are played at Three Cousins. A backstop near the garage is home plate for stickball games, and the pitching rubber is found at the bend in the driveway. If anyone hits the ball over a certain branch in the street at the opposite end of the yard, the drive is a home run. On the roof of the garage is a basketball backboard with a Viking, the Winthrop High mascot, painted on it. A regulation-size hockey net is ready for use, and the trees on the other side of the yard are the field goal posts for football contest.

After graduation from Boston University, Eruzione, like Olympic teammate Buzz Schneider, spent several seasons in the minor leagues. He played for two years with Toledo of the International Hockey League, and was voted American rookie of the year in 1978. The rookie star seemed certain of playing, at least for a short time, in the NHL and signing a pro contract. However, neither happened. John Ferguson, general manager of the New York Rangers, was interested in Eruzione, but he was fired and the new regime of Fred Shero had no plans for the minor leaguer, and he stayed in Toledo.

"I was surprised that he was cut by the Rangers," says O'Brien, Eruzione's high school coach. "I thought somebody in the NHL would realize what a great deal of good he could do for a team, and pick him up. Mike would have been a great checker, maybe on the third line, plus he would have picked up the odd goal and would have been a great person to have in the locker room.

"His personality makes a team happy. He was the perfect leader on our team—very exciting, very lively, very enjoyable to be around."

Eruzione continued to play in Toledo, although he was becoming disenchanted with the game. BU coach, Jack Parker, talked to him about joining his coaching staff, but Eruzione wanted to give hockey another chance, this time with the Olympic team.

Staying on the U.S. club proved to be nearly as difficult as winning a berth on an NHL roster. The team has faster forwards than Eruzione in Eric Strobel, Mark Johnson and Rob McClanahan. Eruzione was afraid he would be one of the six players that had to be cut before the Olympics. There were many long distance calls back to Winthrop during the six-month exhibition road trip. "You could always tell when he had a bad game," Nancy says. "You'd ask him how he was doing and he'd say, 'I could be gone from here tomorrow.' "

While most of his teammates seemed certain to land pro contracts, no NHL teams indicated any interest in Eruzione, even as late as a month before the Olympics. Although he was voted team captain by the players, it was still very possible that he would be one of the last cuts before Lake Placid. Discouraged, Eruzione went home for a visit.

"Our family is a support group," Nancy says. "We don't expect things or push anybody into doing something, but we're always here. If Michael had broken his leg in the Olympics, never scored a goal or hadn't been named to the team, he still would have been a hero to us. I guess you could say our family is like a safety net. We draw strength from each other."

When Eruzione arrived back in Winthrop, his family suggested that he retire from the game. At first Eruzione refused to consider retirement, then, as he thought about it, their proposal made more sense. "I decided two weeks before the Olympics that afterwards I was going back to Toledo and play a month there, just to make some extra money," he says. "Then I was going to go home and start looking for a college coaching job. Then we won the gold medal, and five NHL teams were interested in signing me to a contract. I had all these television appearances to make, and suddenly the decision I had already made started to get all this attention. People were saying, 'I can't believe it.' But if we hadn't won the medal, who would have cared?"

Win a gold medal and everyone becomes your friend, ready and willing to give advice and eat you out of house and home. When the U.S. defeated Finland, there were spontaneous celebrations across the country, and nowhere were the festivities more jubilant than in Winthrop. The afternoon the medals were presented at Lake Placid, people began showing up outside the Eruzione home. They stood on the front lawn and sang "The Star-Spangled Banner" and "God Bless America." As Mike Eruzione talked with the President on the telephone from the U.S. team locker room, Boston's television cameras were pulling up in front of his home on Bowdoin Street. Later, while his family watched Eruzione on the living room TV as he sang the national anthem and then beckoned his teammates to join him atop the victory stand, a stranger in the Eruzione kitchen ate the family's dinner. "I asked him why he was eating our dinner," says Connie, another of Mike's sisters. "He said it was so good, he couldn't resist."

"People were just walking in," Nancy says. "We didn't know hardly any of them."

"One guy walked up to me and said, 'Thanks for having such a great party,' " another sister Annete says. "I told him we weren't having a party."

Other visitors to the Eruzione's that afternoon were an elderly couple from Kenmore Square in Boston. After seeing the U.S. victory, they caught the next bus toward Winthrop. The bus stopped more than a mile away, and they walked the rest of the distance to the Eruzione home. No one was sure who the pair were, but it was assumed they were somebody's relatives. The couple was introduced as Tom and Mary, and they stayed until 1 A.M. talking and drinking, and then were driven home. Later, it was discovered that the pair were not related to the Eruziones.

The excitement in Winthrop did not subside. If anything, it peaked when Mike Eruzione came home. The town planned a parade in his honor, and Eruzione was supposed to ride through Winthrop, waving at the hometown crowd from a Rolls Royce. But people crowded around the car, causing thousands of dollars worth of damage. At one point, as Eruzione neared the Rolls, the cheering was so loud, no one could hear themselves speak. Eruzione noticed a woman right next to him yelling, but could not hear her. Finally he was able to make out the words; "You're standing on my foot!" The local police eventually forced a human wedge around Eruzione and got him through the crowd and out of danger. "People were a bit too excited," Mr. Eruzione says. "They were pushing the Rolls back and forth. For a minute I thought they might tip it over."

Today, Winthrop remains just as proud, though less demonstrative, of its native son. Bumper stickers, many of them homemade, proclaim that this is "The Home of Mike Eruzione." Many store windows in Winthrop display team photos of the U.S. hockey team and in nearly every one, Mike Eruzione sits in the middle of the front row. To his left is coach Herb Brooks and on his right is assistant coach Craig Patrick. Jim Craig and Steve Janaszak, the team's two goalies, sit at either end of the front row. They look like a pair of bookends. The looks on their faces range from stoic glares to refreshing smiles. Nobody looks happier than their captain.

Each member of the team was a captain or a team leader at some point during his career—anywhere from youth hockey to the college ranks, so Eruzione had a difficult task. He had to earn the respect of a group of young men who were each champions in their own right.

"It was hard to feel like a captain on a team like that," Eruzione says. "How do I say to a guy like Jack O'Callahan or Billy Baker that 'You better start getting going, you're not playing well?' I considered myself a captain among captains. Just because I had the "C," I had the dirty job of talking to Herb [Brooks] and maybe saying something in the locker room. But our team never had to be told what they had to do. They were all talented enough hockey players that they knew when and how to get themselves ready for a game.

"If I wanted to have a team meeting, I wouldn't just say 'We're having a team meeting.' I would ask Buzzy (Schneider) 'What do you think?' or Jack (O'Callahan), 'Do you think we can have something like this?' I got opinions on things. I was no dictator."

The Eruzione approach of being understated and understanding worked, and most team members call him the best captain they ever had. He was their friend first, and their captain second. For instance, when many of the players bought gifts for their girlfriends during the weeks before Christmas, the person they often asked to come along and help them out was Eruzione.

"He was a great guy," says John Harrington, "So outgoing and happy. No matter what happened there was always a bright spot when Mike talked about it. He'd find something in our performance that went right and he'd say 'Well, this went right and this went wrong and there's another game coming up, and let's keep working at it.'

"He also would go to Herb with any little problem anyone told him about. Some guys wouldn't go in and talk with Herb, one on one, like that. I don't think I would have. But you just had to say something to Mike and boom, he'd be right up there hammering on the door."

Eruzione was also regarded as a good captain because he had a sense of humor, and could laugh at himself. During the exhibition tour, his mother sent him a copy of a feature story which appeared in a local newspaper. Bill Baker got a hold of the article and read it out loud in the locker room with some assistance from Dave Silk.

PHOTO COURTESY OF BOSTON HERALD

The players, including Eruzione, laughed as the paper detailed their captain's career in glowing plaudits and clichés. The paper retold the story of Eruzione's first time on skates. At the age of seven, Eruzione put on his sister's white figure skates—complete with pom-poms—and walked down to Winthrop Golf Course, a half-block from his home. He climbed over the fence and went out on the ice-covered trap near the seventh green. Eruzione spent the next two winters there learning to skate.

"Back then, at first, trying to get across that distance seemed the most impossible thing in the world," he says. "I had a little hockey stick and a puck and I used to be out there for hours. When I was done I'd walk home—back up the hill, and my grandmother used to open the oven door to thaw out my feet."

Eruzione improved so rapidly that he began playing organized hockey at the age of nine, and, later, after leading Winthrop to its first conference title, he looked forward to playing Division I hockey. No college seemed to want him, however. New Hampshire said he was too small and Boston College said he was too poor a skater. Eruzione was ready to attend Merrimack College, a Division II school, until BU coach Jack Parker noticed him in a summer league game. Parker was officiating the contest and afterwards he asked a couple of Eruzione's friends about his plans. "I was new to the recruiting game back then," Parker says. "I had seen Mike play in bantam and high school, and I was surprised when they told me nobody had given him the opportunity to play Division I."

Parker offered Eruzione a scholarship, and, less than a month before the fall semester began, he enrolled at BU. Four years later, Eruzione was the college's second all-time leading scorer, only one point beyond his good friend Rick Meagher. In addition, he had all but retired the award as the best defensive forward in the Boston area by winning it four consecutive years.

"It's very hard to come in as a freshman and play as well as he did," Parker says. "But what's even more difficult is to keep that going over four years. But Mike had pride in himself and where he is from and that stays with him."

It's mid-afternoon at Logan Airport, and Mike Eruzione strides off another shuttle from New York City. His face is tanned, and he picks his way quickly through the crowd and then makes his usual stop at the airport restaurant to see his sister Jeannie. He talks about the photo session he just completed with actress Jane Alexander. The pair posed for a Boston Magazine cover, and were featured with Ben Bradlee, Mike Wallace and Barbara Walters in a story about

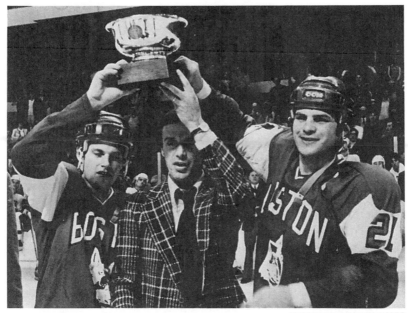

Mike Eruzione (21), BU coach Jack Parker (center) and Rick Meagher hold aloft the first-place trophy after the ECAC title game in March of 1977.

growing up in the Boston area. "You'd have liked Jane Alexander," he tells his sister, who now receives twice as many tips because her last name is Eruzione. "She was a lot of laughs. Looks better in person than she did in the movie *Kramer vs. Kramer*."

Jeannie leaves to wait on another table, and Eruzione mentions a Hollywood party he attended a few weeks before and how a producer asked him if he had thought about being an actor. Eruzione was interested, but the conversation quickly ended when he was informed that most actors live on the West Coast. Eruzione explained that he had no intention of moving that far away from his family in Winthrop.

"You want another beer, Mike?" Jeannie asks, returning to the table.

"No, I'm going home to have some soup and take a nap before dinner," he replies. "I haven't seen everybody since last week. We'll be up all night talking."

CHAPTER 9

The Midas Touch

What's happened to Alfalfa?—Spanky
Oh, he's gone Hollywood.—Buckwheat
—scene from "Our Gang" comedy series

As the U.S. gold medal victory over Finland became history, the American bench emptied onto the ice and the team skated toward its net to congratulate goalie Jim Craig. Some of the players threw sticks and gloves into the crowd in their exuberance, and captain Mike Eruzione retrieved the game puck. Eric Strobel was the first to reach Craig, and he threw his arms around the goalie's neck and hugged him. Buzz Schneider was the next one to pile on, and within seconds there was a mass of humanity around the American net. Neal Broten danced a little jig, while Jack O'Callahan and Mike Ramsey rolled on the ice, their faces in wide grins.

Amid the cheering and commotion, Craig slowly skated away from his teammates and toward the side of the rink, his eyes scanning the stands. Two youngsters climbed over the boards and onto the ice and draped an American flag over the goalie's shoulders. Craig smiled briefly at his two new fans and then looked back toward the crowd. Standing alone, he peered into the cheering throngs. Across the country, millions read his lips as he asked, "Where's my father?" For many television viewers it was the most poignant moment of the Olympics.

Jim Craig found his father minutes later in the hallway to the locker room, and the two embraced and kissed. That afternoon, Mr. Craig looked on as his son received his medal from Lord Killanin, president of the International Olympic Committee. Jim Craig smiled as the crowd applauded, and looked at the piece of gold hanging around his neck. It was a day that months later, he would be hardpressed to describe fully or totally forget he was recognized, at least for that day, as the best goaltender in the world, and his family had been there to enjoy it with him. A total of 18 relatives —brothers, sisters, nieces, and nephews—were with his father up in the stands.

As Craig walked off the presentation platform and turned to watch his teammates, the pin that held the medal to the ribbon around his neck broke, and the gold medal came off in his hands.

PHOTO BY PETE HALPERN

Jim Craig tosses the puck to a stunned referee who cannot figure out how the U.S. goalie kept the last shot out of the net.

The incident was an omen. The Finland game was the last contest Craig played strictly for fun and for his family. Soon, the game would become a business and the Olympic goalie, much to his chagrin, would find himself more of a huckster than a player.

The Atlanta Flames (the team that owned the Olympian's NHL rights) were negotiating a contract with the goalie's agent and within days Craig would be working for them. Atlanta did not need another goalie. The team had veteran Dan Bouchard and young Pat

Riggin. But with home attendance declining and the team about $2 million in the red, the Flames needed someone to promote the team, and Olympic hero Jim Craig fit the bill.

The evening after the Finland game, Craig had a couple of beers and went to bed. Early the next morning, a Monday, he and the rest of the Olympic team flew from Lake Placid to the White House to shake hands with the President. On Tuesday, Craig appeared on the television show "Good Morning, America" with his father, who explained where he was when the U.S. won the gold.

"I had swapped my tickets and was in Section 3," Mr. Craig said. "I wanted to be closer to my boy. Jim couldn't find me. I knew what he was thinking . . . I was so proud and it brought back fond memories It's too bad Jim's mom couldn't be with him. She was his greatest booster."

"All I wanted to do was to make eye contact with him," Jim Craig added. "Then I could relax. I only wish Mom could have been there Sunday to see me get the gold medal." Craig's mother died of cancer in 1977.

Tuesday, Craig landed at Boston's Logan Airport and was greeted by a motorcade which escorted him back to North Easton, Massachusetts. On Wednesday Craig sat atop a fire engine holding his gold medal, and was paraded down Main Street. That evening, the final terms of Craig's contract with the Atlanta Flames were ironed out. A fourth-round draft pick in 1977, Craig signed with the Flames through the 1982-1983 season for a reported $85,000 a year, plus a $45,000 bonus. By Saturday afternoon—after two more press conferences, a couple of dozen interviews, standing ovations on every plane he walked onto and being nicknamed "The Savior" by his pro teammates—the novelty of being a golden boy had worn off.

"I think I've slept about 14 hours since the Olympics," he told one reporter. "I haven't been feeling well, either. I'm taking cough medicine, pills and something for my ulcer. With all the tension, the doctor thinks I have one started." He even admitted that the crowds "have been driving me crazy."

Saturday evening, Craig was dressed in a Flames' jersey and ready to guard the net against the Colorado Rockies. Despite an ice storm that brought Atlanta to a standstill, the Flames had their first sell-out of the season.

Atlanta won the game 4-1, and Craig made enough difficult saves to put together a commercial featuring him. In the locker room after the game, Craig fielded reporters' questions until midnight, as his new teammates slowly dressed and left. Craig and his father worked into the early morning hours, filming the last scene for the commercial. In it the goalie says "Take it from two guys who've had a lot to cheer about lately," and gulps down the bubbling brown liquid. On his left, Mr. Craig looks on, his arm around his son.

The Atlanta Flames' bus pulled up in front of the Hotel Toronto, a plush inn across from City Hall in downtown Toronto. The players filed off and into the lobby. Some, like all-star Garry Unger, wore cowboy hats, and others were dressed in conservative business suits. One of the last to walk off the bus was Jim Craig. He was attired in a team blazer with a red, flaming "A" on his pocket. Many of the Flames collected their room keys from the front desk and went upstairs for another room service dinner and another early evening. This was Craig's first trip to Toronto, and even though it was a cold Sunday evening, he and teammate Kent Nilsson left for a night on the town, beginning with dinner at the Top of Toronto restaurant, one of the city's top tourist attractions.

The hostess smiled a big smile and immediately walked over to the pair of hockey players when they entered.

"You must be Jim Craig," she said. "I saw you looking for your father on TV."

"Yeah, that's me," Craig replied.

"Did you ever find him?"

"Yeah, I did."

The Top of Toronto is the world's highest revolving restaurant and located three-quarters of the way up the CN Tower, a needle-like skyscraper on the Toronto waterfront. It was a clear night, and the expressway of cars stretched like ribbons of light down the shore of Lake Ontario, to Hamilton, Ontario, and the reddish flow of that city's steel factories. The restaurant rotated, and Toronto and its surrounding suburbs were slowly revealed in a haze of twinkling lights.

The setting seemed appropriate for Craig. After all, he was on top of the world, the team hero and a person everyone recognized. But Craig was becoming disenchanted with his role because he played only four games after the Olympics. He spent most games in the pressbox doing interviews, rather than on the ice. Three weeks after the Finland game, it was no longer fun being the celebrity with the golden touch.

In Chicago, one of the few games he was scheduled to dress for, Craig tried to take a nap the afternoon of the game. Before going to sleep he called the switchboard to ask for a wake-up call.

"Wake me up in two hours," he said

"Certainly sir," the operator said. "What's your last name, please?"

"Craig."

"Craig? You're not Jim Craig, are you?"

After a pause, he replied, "Yes, I'm Jim Craig."

"Jim Craig, the hockey player!" the operator exclaimed. "I've just got to meet you. I'll be up a couple of minutes."

"I'm trying to get some sleep," Craig pleaded.

"I just want to say hello. Be right up."

Craig waited for some 10 minutes, and when his visitors didn't show up, he went to bed. From time to time during his nap, Craig woke up with the nagging feeling of being watched. He shrugged it off and went back to sleep. Finally, he became too restless, rolled over and looked around the room. Peeking around the bedroom door were four heads—the switchboard operator and three maids. They giggled and ran out of the room.

"Just goes to show you there's always somebody watching," Craig said later.

Back at the CN Tower, the Top of Toronto spun high above the world below. Donna Summer's "MacArthur Park" played over the sound system, and Craig and Nilsson talked. The conversation, even though it began with the beauty of Atlanta's women, soon shifted to the problems of being a benchwarmer. Since Lake Placid, Craig had signed countless autographs while his teammates played. The goalie wanted to be on the ice, too. He longed for a regular turn in the nets.

"Tomorrow we're playing at Maple Leaf Gardens," Craig said. "I'd love to play there. But from what I know right now, I probably wouldn't even be dressed."

"We've just got too many good goalies now," Nilsson said. "They'll trade somebody, but I don't know who."

"There's no room," Craig said. "You know that what they say about three being a crowd. That's what we got here. They've got (Dan) Bouchard, he's good. And (Pat) Riggin, he's so young that they'll hang onto him. That leaves me out. I need to work to play well. I want to show people that I can play in this league."

"Who knows, Jimmy, maybe they'll trade you to Boston," Nilson said.

"I'd like that," Craig said softly. "It would be nice to go back home."

Forty-five minutes south of Boston, over rolling hills and past an occasional mansion, is the sleepy village of North Easton. Five homes in the area were designed by H. H. Richardson, a prominent 19th Century architect, and many of the surrounding estates and parks were landscaped by Frederick Law Olmstead, whose most famous project is New York's Central Park. Up North Main Street, at least a mile from the nearest mansion, is the modest home of Don Craig and his family.

While his son traveled around the country after the Olympics, Mr. Craig stayed at home, answering a telephone that refused to stop ringing, and sorting the mail. Phone calls to the Craig household numbered more than 50 a day, and the morning mail swelled from a few letters to several sackfuls. Sitting at his kitchen table, Mr. Craig opens it all and divides it into categories—kids, adults, organizations and women. The last group of letters and requests, Jim Craig seldom sees. His father opens them, shakes his head and files such solicitations away in large manilla envelopes and hides them in a back room.

"We've gotten them from all over," Mr. Craig says. "Some girls think he's just the cutest thing. Some of these I'm embarrassed to even read. Take a look at this one."

It's a letter from a brunette beauty in Dallas, complete with photographs of the woman in several suggestive poses. Her resume includes measurements, favorite sports, likes and dislikes—a Playboy-style rundown of personal data.

"Now that kind of stuff wouldn't do Jim any good at all," Mr. Craig says.

Though the advances from gorgeous women make up a large chunk of Jim Craig's post-Olympic mail, the majority of correspondence comes from children and male adults. The letters from kids are often in crayon, and many ask for an autograph. They are cute, humorous, and Mr. Craig will often look through hundreds a day. The letters from parents are even more moving.

"I'm the father of three sons and a daughter, and I live in a society suffering from alienation of family," a man from Moorhead, Minnesota, wrote. "The only hope is that when my sons reach Jim's age that our relationship will be so strong that when they yearn for companionship either during suffering or celebration that they will still cherish their relationship with their parents. Your son has provided us with an inspiring example for fathers everywhere."

"Just imagine this, a whole family getting up early on Sunday morning for the game," wrote a young man from Garden City, New York. "We were all dressed in red, white and blue. My father and I hung the flag outside for this special occasion."

"When I was 11 and beginning to dream about becoming a priest, the American hockey team at Squaw Valley won the gold and made us all proud," wrote a priest from Massachusetts. "Now, twenty years later, you've rekindled that same pride . . ."

One of the most touching was a cassette tape from a middle-aged man in New Jersey. "This tape is a personal thing between you and me, Jim," he said. "I was ashamed of being an American. My pride was eroded. . . . When the team won and you said 'Where's my father?' I broke down and cried. . . . Thanks for letting me see the good side of our country again. Thank you for making me proud to be an American."

Mr. Craig responds to all the letters with the same honesty and emotion in which they were written. After the Olympics, he bought 300 stamps to use for his reply. A couple of weeks later they were all gone. "I'm going to get back to all these people," he says. "Even if it takes me a couple of years."

The Craig home is not a Richardson-Olmstead creation, but it's picturesque and a great deal more practical for prospective hockey stars. In back of the house is a shallow pond. Trees grow in the water: only the base of their trunks and their roots are under water. In time, the trees and accompanying vegetation will conquer, and the pond will become a marsh and then a meadow. But when Jim Craig was learning to skate, the area was a pond.

"The first time I went down to the pond I was nine years old," Craig says. "They wouldn't let me play hockey because I was too little, and besides, I was wearing figure skates. I didn't have anything else, and when you're one of eight kids you don't get a pair of hockey skates like that."

Unable to play with the big boys, Craig and his friends designed obstacle courses and raced in between the trees. Craig contends that is why he is such a good skater today. The next year he received his first pair of hockey skates and started playing goal.

"I borrowed them from a neighbor," Craig says. "Couldn't even sharpen them in the sharpening machine because they were a different type of blade, a real soft blade. The shoes had soft toes, and when it got wet they would bend in. The eyelets popped out, so I had to tape them back on and I played goal like that for a while, until my dad bought me some of my own stuff."

Throughout grade and high school, Craig was small for his age, measuring only 5'6" when he graduated from high school. Four years later, in the Olympics, he stood 6'1". Despite being shorter than most of his teammates while a kid, Craig excelled in hockey. Oliver Ames High School won 53 games and lost only four with him in the nets. His first year out of high school, Craig led Massasoit Community College to a small college championship, and then decided he wanted to play Division I hockey. Boston University offered him a scholarship, and the school met one of Craig's re-

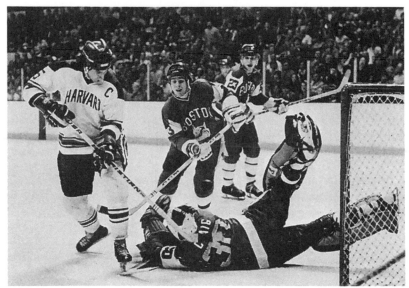

BOSTON UNIVERSITY PHOTO

Jim Craig makes the save during the 1977 Beanpot game against Harvard at the Boston Garden.

quirements—it was close to home. However, the Terriers already had a proven goalie in Brian Durocher, and Craig wanted to play. BU coach Jack Parker assured Craig that he only played his best goalie and did not have a seniority system at BU. Craig surprised everybody, including Parker, with his play and by mid-season he was the No. 1 goalie.

While Jim Craig battled for a starting job, his mother fought for her life. She was in the hospital for long periods of time that year, being treated for bone cancer, and she missed many of her son's games.

"I remember when he heard that she had gone into the hospital for what was the last time," says BU coach Jack Parker. "We had won, and Jim played and the team was back in the locker room when he found out. He got very quiet.

"Jim never said much about his mother, but it affected him. She came to all his games. Now, when he looked up, she wasn't there."

On September 1977, weighing only 47 pounds, Margaret Craig died. Her son Jim dedicated the following season to her memory.

Craig had an undefeated record that year and played an outstanding game against crosstown rival Boston College in the NCAA final. BU won the game, 5-3, to take the title.

"After Lake Placid we got a lot of letters from many of Jim's teachers and teammates at BU," Mr. Craig says. "I think they were just as proud and happy as we were."

Although he is 61 years old, Don Craig's features are still well-defined, and his body as trim as an athlete's. Baseball was the elder Craig's first sports love. In 1936, he worked at Ames Shovel and Tool Company in Easton while he made up his mind whether to try out for a pro team or accept a scholarship to play college baseball. But his hand was crushed in a vise, ending his dream of a baseball career. Now the only time he picks up a baseball is to play catch in the backyard with his sons.

From his family, Mr. Craig receives love and respect. Earlier in the day, a five-year-old granddaughter visited him. When her mother came to pick her up, the child kissed her grandfather good-bye before walking out the door. Everyone in the Craig family kisses the "old man" farewell before leaving the house.

"Some people ask if Jim and I are queer because I kiss him after each game," Mr. Craig says. "But that's a stupid question. It's just important that we know the other one is there. He kisses me before leaving the house just like the little ones do. They all do."

After putting the last of the letters away in a back room, Mr. Craig leads the way into the living room, stops for a moment and takes a quick glance around the room. "I don't let the little ones in here," he says. "There's too many fragile things."

An organ stands against the far wall, its keys covered. The curtains are open and through the windows, the trees down near the pond can be seen. The room contains some hockey awards Jim Craig and his brothers have won, but most of that paraphernalia is displayed in the TV room. On the living room wall is the painting of a woman. She is middle-aged, and there still is the fresh beauty of a young girl in her face, especially around the eyes and mouth. The painting, and the sunlight streaming in through the window, fills the room with a warm glow. The painting is of Jim Craig's mother, Margaret. When Craig was a child, his mother drove him to most of his games, was his best fan and kept telling him that even short people can be stars in the NHL. Whenever Craig returns to North Easton one of his first stops is the local cemetary to visit with his mother. Craig says they still talk to each other. "She can still burn my ears off," he claims. During the Olympics, Craig assured his father that everything was going to work out because his mother was looking out for him and the team.

"I guess there's one last thing I should show you," Mr. Craig says, turning away from the portrait. "It's the only thing Jim ever bought for his room. Jim is not the type to spend money. I guess you'd say he's a loner. He doesn't need a lot of people. But he did want this."

Up the stairs and to the right is Craig's bedroom, now the domain of a younger brother. The room is on the same side of the house as the living room. Tacked to a closet door is a poem. The verse begins,

"Here is a man without desire,
   Here is a man without purpose in life,
Here is a fool . . ."

Fourteen lines later, the poem closes with a thought that best represents the Craig family and its home in North Easton.

"Today lasts a fraction of minute,
   Yesterday lasted an Eternity.
And having lasted an Eternity
   I can say that,
I truely lived a fruitful life,
   One of everlasting love."

Several days after the 1979-80 NHL playoffs ended, the Flames traded their Olympic goalie to the Boston Bruins for two draft choices. Jim Craig's promotional tour was drawing to a close. He was going home.

CHAPTER 10

The Best of Both Worlds

You don't have to be angry to be a good hockey player.

— Eric Heiden

Standing a strapping 6'4" and with a coal-black beard, he looks like Abe Lincoln in a hockey uniform. Pass him a stove-top hat and you expect him to begin reciting the Gettysburg Address. And the comparison goes even further than looks. One was a presidential hope for a Union. The other is the American prospect for the NHL, the leader of the Olympic pack that has moved into the big leagues. One stood firm against the Confederates. The other quietly keeps rebel forwards from mounting a threat on goal.

Let the others scramble up and down the ice, frequently out of position. It's OK, because Ken Morrow, the bearded one, will be ready when the unguarded winger bursts into the clear. He will poke the puck off the forward's blade with a sweeping motion of his stick and then effectively nudge the forward into the boards. The play rarely brings the fans out of their seats, but later, on the bench, a teammate will lean over and say to the bearded defenseman, "Thanks for covering up for me, Mo."

Off the ice, Morrow remains out of the spotlight. Sitting quietly in front of his stall in the corner of the New York Islanders' locker room, he watches the reporters buzz around, going from one player to another like so many bees after honey. When pressed for a comment, he will smile and speak a few words in a low soothing voice. Then he will smile again and go back to dressing. He removes an ice pack from his shoulder. The joint is still sore, slightly separated at the Olympiad. After wiping the water off his shoulders and chest, he searches the floor for his boots. Finding them he pulls them over his white tube socks that bear the inscription "Lake Placid Olympics."

"I never dreamed about the gold medal or the Olympics as a kid," he says, looking up from his feet. "I didn't even begin to think about the Olympics until my last year of school at Bowling Green. I heard that I had a pretty good chance of making the team, so I went out. I guess if I dreamed about anything as a kid it was the Stanley Cup."

On the top slate of his stall is a piece of adhesive tape with the name "Ken Morrow" scribbled on it with black magic marker. Perhaps the temporary nameplate should also have a gold star on it,

PHOTO COURTESY OF NEW YORK ISLANDERS

Ken Morrow

because it fails to mention that Morrow was hockey's most triumphant hockey player of 1980 as he became the first person ever to win an Olympic gold medal and help win the Stanley Cup in the same year.

On May 24, 1980—exactly three months after the U.S. win at Lake Placid—the bearded defenseman was involved in another celebration as the New York Islanders won the first league championship of their history. In the victorious locker room, the questions began, "Which is the biggest thrill?" "What award are you most proud of?" Morrow just looked up at the crowd of reporters standing around him and said, "I don't think it's fair to compare the two." It's a reply he had prepared ahead of time.

Amid the champagne and revelry of the Islanders' win, the most important point of Morrow's accomplishment was overlooked. The fact that the reserved unassuming defenseman was even on a big league roster may be an indication that the NHL is finally cleaning up its act. During the Seventies, the league was infamous for its unimaginative offenses and premeditated outbursts of violence. However, with the arrival of the U.S. Olympians, the NHL has a golden opportunity to improve its game by incorporating some of the grace and elegance of American hockey.

The XIII Olympiad demonstrated that a substantial new audience awaited the league if it began playing a more wide-open style and forgot about violence. The television ratings for the U.S.-Soviet Union and U.S.-Finland games were nearly 40 million, and certainly a large percentage of those viewers were only interested in seeing the Russians defeated or the Americans clinch the gold medal. However, many were newcomers to the game, and liked what they saw. To them hockey was a fast-paced sport played by interesting people. The athletes were not thugs out beating their opponents and a piece of hard rubber into submission. The body-checks were thrown, but except for isolated incidents, they were clean hits.

For too many years, the NHL has emphasized fighting and brawls in an attempt to sell its game. The sales pitch boomeranged and serious sports fans thought the league a joke. The NHL lost its national television contract at the conclusion of the 1974-75 season. The contests currently shown on TV are broadcast by cable or local stations. The U.S. hockey team played a different kind of game, and drew such responses from all parts of the country that network executives considered putting the sport back on the tube. "If that happens, it won't be because the NHL suddenly came out of the Stone Age;" wrote the Chicago Tribune's Gary Deeb in his television column, "it'll be because a bunch of gritty American college kids played their hearts out and sold the sport to millions of armchair viewers across the country."

Besides Morrow, Olympic heroes like Dave Christian (Winnipeg Jets), Steve Christoff (Minnesota North Stars), Jim Craig (Atlanta Flames), Mark Johnson (Pittsburgh Penguins), Rob McClanahan and Mike Ramsey (Buffalo Sabers) signed NHL contracts within two weeks of the final buzzer of Lake Placid. Some NHL players, like Buffalo's Rick Dudley, think the Olympians will help change the game for the better. "If the kids from the Olympics prove to be effective in the NHL then that will allow for more skaters," he says. "For such a long time it was thought that it wasn't exciting enough to just have a bunch of skaters. But if there's one thing the whole Olympics proved, especially with all the attention on the American team, is that this is a skating game and people will watch that."

Ken Morrow in action as a New York Islander.

Others are more skeptical. They claim that the U.S. victory will have little effect on the professional game because many members of the NHL establishment are too stubborn and too inflexible to change their ways.

"I doubt if a single series like the Olympics is going to wake anybody up," says Howie Meeker, former NHL player and now a commentator for Hockey Night In Canada. "I'd love to see more skating and passing in the pro game, but I don't think it's here yet. You still see too many teams in this league shoot the puck in, even when they have a three-on-two or two-on-two break. That's a waste of time and effort."

None of the Olympians who jumped from the U.S. hockey team to the NHL are eager to talk about their new roles. Many wonder if they are changing the game or being altered by it, and some are receiving a quick initiation in fights, butt ends and cheap shots. "Let's just call it a real eye-opener," says Rob McClanahan. "Nobody passes up a hit in this league."

The Olympic hero who is convinced that the new stars will make a difference is Ken Morrow. "I think our victory helped hockey," he contends.

"I enjoyed the big rinks at Lake Placid," Morrow adds. "I think it was a little better game because you didn't see the low-scoring, tight-checking kind of games that you see in the NHL. The Olympics also let a player use his abilities more and show off his stick-handling and skating. I wouldn't call the game (in the NHL) boring, but it is a little different."

A classic example of this difference was illustrated the night the U.S. defeated the Soviet Union. The Russian squad was essentially the same one that defeated the NHL all-stars the year before in the Challenge Cup series. While the Americans were beating the Soviets with outstanding goaltending, exciting skating and a lot of heart, the NHL was putting on a characteristic display of all that is wrong with its game. The Philadelphia Flyers defeated the Vancouver Canucks 7-3, and, along the way, 16 players were ejected and play was stopped for 45 minutes for a bench-clearing brawl. More than 300 minutes in penalties were called, compared to only 12 minutes in the U.S.-C.C.C.P. contest.

Such incidents as the Flyer-Canucks riot begin with the poor attitude of the NHL management. Following the U.S. gold medal victory over Finland, league president John Ziegler dismissed the Olympic brand of hockey. "I'm not all that concerned with the style that teams in our league use," he wrote in Hockey News, the supposed bible for fans, "mainly because I don't think the European style of hockey can sell and be good entertainment for 1,000 games year, which is what we are faced with in the NHL." Somebody should show him the Olympic television ratings.

Several weeks later, at the NHL's Lester Patrick dinner in New York, where the U.S. team was presented with an award for outstanding service to hockey, the great debate continued. Since the Americans had come home with the gold, coach Brooks had publicly maintained that his players were exceptional because they accepted being hit. When Americans got an elbow in the jaw or a stick in the face, they rarely retaliated by dropping their gloves and starting a fight. Penalties were costly in Olympic play, especially against the power plays of the Swedes, Czechs and Russians, and fisticuffs resulted in players being thrown out of the games. The U.S. team, unlike many NHL squads, remained patient and did not lose its temper. "The team accepted being bounced around," Brooks said. "We showed our tenaciousness, toughness and our heart by accepting being hit. We had a couple of fights [during the exhibition season], but that was not by design. That was not part of our game plan.

"I think the Olympic style of hockey works because it gives players a chance to bring out their natural abilities," Brooks continued, as the group of listeners grew in size. "I've got a lot of respect for the players in the National Hockey League, just as I did for the players on the Olympic team. If I didn't I wouldn't have given them this new system, and we would have been playing kitty-bar-the-door hockey up at Lake Placid."

Several listeners were still cynical of American hockey, even after Brooks' soliloquy. The argument lasted until Brooks asked Bobby Clarke, former captain of the Philadelphia Flyers, what he thought. Surprisingly, Clark replied: "I agree with you, Herb." In the mid-Seventies, the Flyers were a rowdy, brawling team, nicknamed the Broad Street Bullies. Clarke, the team's leader, was once quoted as saying, "If they cut down on violence too much, people won't come out to watch. It's a reflection of our society."

Even though the great hockey debate continued, little was immedately resolved, and the ugliness of the professional game again became apparent. Olympian John Harrington, a former member of the Iron Ranger line, decided to play with Rochester, a farm team for the Buffalo Sabres, after the Olympics were over. He soon became disillusioned with the game on the minor-league level. In his first professional game, he witnessed a bench-clearing brawl and in a subsequent contest he picked up six stitches in the chin after being slashed with a stick. Such incidents were minor compared to what happened next. In a game against rival Hershey, Harrington was checked in the back of the head by Lou Franceschetti. The blow knocked Harrington unconscious, and he fell face-first on the ice. The result was a concussion, a broken nose and several loose teeth. No penalty was called on the play. "It was a cheap shot," Rochester winger Paul Crowley reportedly said, "Franceschetti didn't have to ram his nose into the ice."

"How did I get it in the back of my head if it was a clean shot?" Harrington asks. "There are guys in this league that are just hanging on when they can't do it talent-wise. In international hockey they challenge you with talent. In this league if they can't keep up, they slow you down any way they can."

Although Olympians like Ken Morrow, Rob McClanahan and others think the NHL will eventually become a better place for skaters, many of their U.S. teammates decided they wanted no part of North American hockey. Buzz Schneider and Mark Pavelich signed contracts with teams in Switzerland. Eric Strobel and John Harrington also contemplated moving their game to Europe. Mike Eruzione turned down five NHL offers to retire from the game. Phil Verchota, instead of playing for the Minnesota North Stars, went back to college. And Bob Suter opened a sports shop in Madison, Wisconsin.

"A lot of the guys grew up playing a cleaner game," Schneider says. "Where I played high school hockey there weren't many fights, just some pushing and shoving, the same in college at 'the U.' I got used to that skating kind of game."

NHL hockey should be the same. Talented players like Schneider, Pavelich and Strobel are showmen on the ice and the reason why many watched the sport during the Olympics. Their play is choreographed in deft movements, a dance performed in colorful jerseys against a white background of ice. But, there is no immediate place in the NHL for these Olympians and the play of the league's own stars like Guy Lafleur and Marcel Dionne is often lost in boring play and violent tactics. During the Seventies, the on-ice antics were so rampant that the violence became a threat to a player's well-being and soon came under the scrutiny of the law. Toronto's Maple Leaf Gardens, once the showcase for gentlemanly players like Dave Keon and Murray Oliver, became the setting for a confrontation with the courts.

During a televised game in 1975, former Detroit Red Wing Dan Maloney jumped Toronto's Brian Glennie from behind, wrestled him to the ice and began slugging him. Finally, grabbing the prostrate Glennie by the shoulders, Maloney slammed the Toronto defenseman's head against the ice. Outraged by such violence at the Gardens, Ontario attorney general Roy McMurtry charged Maloney under the section of the Canadian Criminal Code that states "everyone who unlawfully causes bodily harm to any person" can be brought to court—regardless of whether the culprit wears a hockey jersey. The court found Maloney not guilty, although the jury declared that steps should be taken to avoid "any such occurrence in the future." While the charges against Maloney caused some rumblings, McMurtry made headlines in the Philadelphia-Toronto playoff series in April 1976 when several players ended up in the stands fighting with Leafs and fans. The attorney general charged Bob Kelly, Joe Watson, Don Saleski and Mel Bridgman of the Flyers with assault and possession of a deadly weapon—a hockey stick. The maximum penalty for each offense is five years in prison. Watson and Kelly pleaded guilty and were fined $750 and $200 respectively. Charges against Saleski and Bridgman were later dropped. "That series," McMurtry says, "crossed the fine line and became nothing more than a dimension of criminality."

Even after such episodes and the Lake Placid victory, some NHL owners say the league must permit fighting as a release for player frustration. Many, like all-star Marcel Dionne, think such talk is ridiculous. "They still think that fighting sells tickets, and they are not inspired to use different ways to play the game," he said after the U.S. hockey win. "I've said many things in the past about violence in this league, and even if we had a unanimous agreement among the players, we would still have to play within the guidelines offered by the owners. We signed the contract, we are the ones who must fit in."

With the increased American participation, there was also growing evidence that the NHL's violence problem was rooted in the traditional Canadian way of producing pro players. As the Seventies drew to a close, the majority of NHL players were Canadian, although the level of Americans in the league was growing. In 1975, U.S. athletes made up less than two percent of the NHL. In the days immediately after the 1980 Olympics, that figure grew to more than 11 percent.

Canadian and American youngsters begin their hockey dream in much the same way—a puck, a pair of used skates, a stick whittled down to size and a sheet of ice. Ken Morrow began skating on a small pond in his backyard. He helped his father, Don, and his older brother, Greg, erect four-foot boards around the rink and put up floodlights so they could skate at night. The rink was used in the early winter mornings and after dinner, and each morning Morrow and his brother hosed down the ice surface before leaving for school.

The story is much the same for nearly every Canadian kid who grows up wanting to play in the NHL. Like Morrow, they dream of someday winning an NHL championship. A few steps below the NHL, though, the two nations take divergent paths to the top. Canadian youngsters leave home in their mid-teens and join a junior team. The players are paid living expenses and are on their own. They can be traded from one junior club to another and it's common for some to play on three different teams during their junior careers.

Many of the problems in violence the NHL faces begin on the Canadian junior level. A study by Jean Poupart, a criminologist at Montreal University's School of Criminology and a hockey fan, indicates that Canadian players are encouraged to be violent by the management of junior teams. Poupart studied amateur players in the Quebec Major League from 1974 to 1976, and interviewed 39 of them at length. Most brought up the violent nature of the sport, and all said they were less aggressive on the ice before they entered the league. Poupart concluded that the major reason for the increased violence was economics. Many of the league's teams were strapped for funds and the owners found that a fast, inexpensive way to draw a crowd was to have mayhem on the ice.

"Canadian lads can still skate with the best of them,"McMurtry says, "but the skills, learning to handle the puck, taking a pass, aren't being taught in our minor hockey. The current hockey setup encourages immaturity."

Meanwhile, American kids usually stay at home, playing for high school or local junior teams until they move on to college. Morrow was a member of the Detroit Junior Red Wings. He and Mark Wells, (later to be teammates at Bowling Green and the Olympic team) led the Junior Red Wings to the national title in 1975.

Detroit is some 60 miles away from Morrow's hometown of Davison, Michigan, and his father, an assembly-line worker, spent many of his evenings driving his two sons to games in the Detroit area. A hockey coach, Mr. Morrow watched his sons play, and on the way back home they would discuss the game over hamburgers in some fast-food joint along Route 15 or Interstate 75. Upon graduation from high school, Morrow decided to remain out of the Canadian junior leagues and play at Bowling Green. He played four seasons there and was named to the Central Collegiate Hockey Association all-star team each year, and was the league's most valuable player his senior year. Under coach Ron Mason, Morrow worked on his offensive moves and scored 34 goals while in college. Unlike his Canadian contemporaries, Morrow had little reason to practice uppercuts and jabs because in the CCHA, as in most U.S. college leagues, a player is ejected from that game and the next contest for fighting.

Ken Morrow as he looked at Bowling Green.

At the end of his sophomore year, Morrow was selected in the fourth round of the 1976 amateur draft by the New York Islanders. The draft that year was noteworthy because it marked the first time in several years that the NHL teams went after good skaters, instead of big aggressive hulks. Only the year before, the top pick had been chippy, enforcer-type players like Mel Bridgman and Kim Clackson. But in 1976, the NHL went for fleet, mobile players like Bill Baker and Reed Larson.

If Morrow had entered the NHL in the mid-Seventies, it's likely that he would have been made into an enforcer. At 6'4", 210 pounds, he certainly is big enough for the role. However, when Morrow joined the NHL in February 1980, Islanders' general manager Bill Torrey and coach Al Arbour told the Olympic defenseman to play his game and to leave the fisticuffs to his teammates. The American fitted in so well that the Islanders traded defenseman Dave Lewis and forward Billy Harris to Los Angeles for center Butch Goring. The deal gave New York two high-scoring centers (Goring and all-star Bryan Trottier) and the depth to outskate Buffalo and Philadelphia for the Stanley Cup.

The other NHL clubs that drafted Olympic stars were just as pleasantly surprised as the Islanders. In Minnesota, Steve Christoff, after scoring only two goals in the Olympics, set a rookie scoring mark in the playoffs with eight goals. In Boston, Jim Craig was billed as the Bruin goalie of the future and heir apparent to Gerry Cheevers. In Buffalo, general manager Scotty Bowman says Mike Ramsey is the "cornerstone" of the Sabre defense in the Eighties. In Winnipeg, Dave Christian scored a goal on his first shift in the NHL and Jets' general manager John Ferguson calls him "the best player on my team."

A couple of weeks following the gold medal ceremony at Lake Placid, Winnipeg was in Toronto to play the Leafs. After checking into the hotel and attending practice, one of Christian's next stops was the Canadian Hockey Hall of Fame. For nearly an hour, the Jets' rookie walked among the glass showcases, looking at the trophies, sticks and awards. On his way out of the building he stopped next to the largest case and gazed at the Stanley Cup. "Someday I'll carry that around the rink," he said to nobody in particular.

Those who signed NHL contracts are no longer going for the gold. Instead their new ambition is to be like Olympic teammate Ken Morrow and drink from Stanley's silver cup. In chasing this dream, maybe they will put a grand old game back on the right path.

CHAPTER 11

A Modern Myth

*Fame is a vapor, popularity is an accident and money
takes wings. The only thing that endures is character.*

—Anonymous

There are many championships awarded every year. The World
Series, the Super Bowl, Indianapolis 500, Wimbledon, the NBA
playoffs, the Masters, the Stanley Cup and the NCAA championships—each has its thrilling moments and superstars. Although
these events cause great excitement, within a few days they have
faded like yesterday's newspaper clippings. But the U.S. hockey
team was somehow different. Its essence lives on far after the final
game has been won and the medals awarded. Played on the grand
scale of the Olympics, the upset wins united the nation. We wish
they were still together—suited up and ready to bring us out of our
chairs with another come-from-behind victory. Many who watched
the Olympics have never been closer to a hockey player than their
television screen. Yet, we felt like we were there, a part of it all as the
team acted out a story line that seemed too good to be true.

A band of youngsters and cast-offs, the U.S. hockey team resembled Jason and the Argonauts, George Washington and his Revolu-
tionary Army, and King Arthur and his Knights of the Round Table
as they reenacted the most popular myth known to humanity:
departure, transformation, return. This three-stage theme has
dominated stories, legends and history since civilization began. The
myth is present in such diverse works as Grimm's fairy tales, the
Bible, Shakespeare's plays and the movie "Star Wars."

The first step for any hero or heroes is a journey into the unknown. The world is again one of boundless opportunity, with
failure always close at hand. The hockey team that gathered at JFK
airport in September 1979 was excited as well as apprehensive of
what the next five months would reveal. The world tests each of us,
and it often breaks us, whether of not we are deserving of its graces.
During the months on the road, virtually everyone on the American
team realized that their initiation into the international style of play
would only come about after hours of work and disappointment.
The failings of each player were pointed out and many became
frustrated in their inability to immediately adapt to the new game. If
the hero carries on, though, he is often befriended by a mentor who

offers ways to win the difficult confrontations to come. King Arthur had Merlin, Luke Skywalker had Ben Kenobi, and the U.S. team had Herb Brooks. Even though his players disliked him, the American coach taught his squad tactics that befuddled their opponents. "The line-up of the 1980 Olympic champions—not so impressive," wrote Anatoli Tarasov, one of the founders of Soviet hockey. "A couple of classy defensemen, about five individually strong forwards—and that is all. But the trump card of the U.S. team this time was its coach, Herb Brooks."

At the end of his initiation, the hero is ready for the ultimate challenge. The task can be as frightening as slaying a dragon or as impossible as defeating the Russians in hockey. However, if the hero is courageous, determined and remembers what he has been taught, the victory will be his and the dream will come true. For generations we have cheered such triumphs—Jason reclaims the Golden Fleece, Shakespeare's Prince Hal becomes King Henry V or a bunch of young Americans win a gold medal.

The final step for the hero is the return home. Upon his arrival he is rewarded for his valor: celebrations and parades are held in his honor. Legend tells us that when the hero steps down from the victory platform, the world is filled with a new energy. We gaze in awe at the grandeur of his achievement and dream of what great deeds we could accomplish. We again have hope.

PART III

Statistical Review

PHOTO BY PETE HALPERN

USA EXHIBITION SCHEDULE

USA 8 Holland Nationals 1 (W)
USA 11 Holland Nationals 4 (W)
USA 1 Reipas (Finland) 2 (L)
USA 4 Saipa (Finland) 1 (W)
USA 6 Sapko (Finland) 0 (W)
USA 5 Karpat (Finland) 4 (W)
USA 5 Lukko (Finland) 3 (W)
USA 1 Jokerit (Finland) 4 (L)
USA 3 Norway Nationals 3 (T)
USA 9 Norway Nationals 0 (W)
USA 2 Minnesota North Stars 4 (L)
USA 1 St. Louis Blues 9 (L)
USA 1 Atlanta Flames 6 (L)
USA 4 Washington Caps 5 (L)
USA 4 Maine Mariners 2 (W)
USA 7 Canada 2 (W)
USA 6 Canada 0 (W)
USA 7 Salt Lake City 5 (W)
USA 10 Colorado College 1 (W)
USA 4 Univ. of Minn-Duluth 0 (W)
USA 8 Univ. of Minnesota 2 (W)
USA 1 Indianapolis 0 (W)
USA 15 Flint 0 (W)
USA 5 Birmingham 2 (W)
USA 3 Houston 4 (L)
USA 6 Birmingham 4 (W)
USA 5 Harvard 0 (W)
USA 9 RPI 3 (W)
USA 3 Cincinnati 2 (W)
USA 6 Salt Lake City 4 (W)
USA 6 Canada 7 (L)
USA 2 Canada 6 (L)
USA 3 Canada 4 (L)
USA 1 Canada 2 (L)
USA 6 Cincinnati 1 (W)
USA 6 North Dakota 1 (W)
USA 5 Oklahoma City 3 (W)
USA 6 Yale 1 (W)
USA 0 Adirondack 1 (L)

PREOLYMPIC TOURNAMENT

USA 4 Sweden 2 (W)
USA 3 Canada 1 (W)
USA 3 Czechoslovakia 0 (W)
USA 5 Russia 3 (W)

EXHIBITION SCHEDULE

USA 4 Gorki Torpedo 2 (W)
USA 5 Gorki Torpedo 1 (W)
USA 10 Gorki Torpedo 3 (W)
USA 2 Indianapolis 2 (T)
USA 2 Gorki Torpedo 3 (L)
USA 4 Oklahoma City 3 (W)
USA 5 Tulsa 2 (W)
USA 5 Houston 3 (W)
USA 7 Tulsa 4 (W)
USA 6 Univ. of Wisconsin 2 (W)
USA 3 Fort Worth 4 (L)
USA 4 Dallas 3 (W)
USA 4 IHL All-Stars 4 (T)
USA 4 Univ. of Wisconsin 2 (W)
USA 3 Fort Worth 5 (L)
USA 10 Dallas 6 (W)
USA 10 Warroad Lakers 0 (W)
USA 3 Russia 10

Record—42-16-3

Individual Statistics

Player	GP	G	A	TP	PIM
Mark Johnson	52	33	48	81	25
Rob McClanahan	55	29	33	62	36
Steve Christoff	56	35	26	61	22
Neal Broten	54	25	30	55	20
Mark Pavelich	52	15	30	45	12
Dave Silk	48	10	33	43	32
Mike Eruzione	42	18	23	41	20
Eric Strobel	48	14	24	38	22
Phil Verchota	53	16	22	38	48
Jack O'Callahan	49	7	29	36	83
Buzz Schneider	54	22	12	34	44
Mike Ramsey	55	11	22	33	55
John Harrington	50	14	18	31	14
Dave Christian	58	10	20	30	26
Bill Baker	52	4	25	29	70
Ralph Cox	31	13	13	26	27
Ken Morrow	55	4	18	22	6
Bob Suter	30	7	11	18	61
Jack Hughes	49	3	15	18	62
Les Auge	29	0	14	14	14
Mark Wells	21	7	6	13	2
Gary Ross	12	1	6	7	4
Dave Delich	13	4	2	6	4
Tim Harrer	4	1	3	4	0
Jim Craig	40	0	3	3	26
Steve Janaszak	16	0	1	1	0
bench	—	—	—	—	8
Totals		303	487	790	733

Goalies	GP	W-L-T	G.A.A.
Jim Craig	40	30-8-1	2.33
Steve Janaszak	16	9-5-1	2.84
Bruce Horsch	9	3-3-1	3.66
Totals		42-16-3	2.60

Olympic Standings
Round Robin Segment
BLUE DIVISION

	W	L	T	Pts	GF	GA
Sweden	4	0	1	9	26	7
United States	4	0	1	9	25	10
Czechoslovakia	3	2	0	6	34	15
Romania	1	3	1	3	13	29
West Germany	1	4	0	2	21	30
Norway	0	4	1	1	9	36

RED DIVISION

	W	L	T	Pts	GF	GA
Soviet Union	5	0	0	10	51	11
Finland	3	2	0	6	26	18
Canada	3	2	0	6	28	12
Poland	2	3	0	4	15	23
Holland	1	3	1	3	16	43
Japan	0	4	1	1	7	36

Tuesday Feb. 12
Sweden 2, United States 2, tie
Czechoslovakia 11, Norway 0
Romania 6, West Germany 4
Soviet Union 16, Japan 0
Canada 10, Holland 1
Poland 5, Finland 4

Thursday, Feb. 14
Sweden 8, Romania 0
West Germany 10, Norway 4
Soviet Union 17, Holland 4
Canada 5, Poland 1
Finland 6, Japan 3
United States 7, Czechoslovakia 3

Saturday, Feb. 16
United States 5, Norway 1
Czechoslovakia 7, Romania 2
Holland 3, Japan 3, tie
Soviet Union 8, Poland 1
Sweden 5, West Germany 2
Finland 4, Canada 3

Monday, Feb. 18
Canada 6, Japan 0
Sweden 7, Norway 1
Holland 5, Poland 3
Soviet Union 4, Finland 2
Czechoslovakia 11, West Germany 3
United States 7, Romania 2

Wednesday, Feb. 20
Romania 3, Norway 3, tie
Sweden 4, Czechoslovakia 1
Poland 5, Japan 1
Soviet Union 6, Canada 4
Finland 10, Holland 3
United States 4, West Germany 2

STANDINGS
MEDALS ROUND

	W	L	T	Pts	GF	GA
United States	2	0	1	5	10	7
Soviet Union	2	1	0	4	16	8
Sweden	0	1	2	2	7	14
Finland	0	2	1	1	7	11

Friday, Feb. 22
United States 4, Soviet Union 3
Sweden 3, Finland 3, tie

Sunday, Feb. 24
United States 4, Finland 2
Soviet Union 9, Sweden 2

Fifth-place Game
Czechoslovakia 6, Canada 1

GOLD MEDAL—United States
SILVER MEDAL—Soviet Union
BRONZE MEDAL—Sweden

FINAL RANKINGS

1. United States
2. Soviet Union
3. Sweden
4. Finland
5. Czechoslovakia
6. Canada
7. Poland
8. Romania
9. Holland
10. West Germany
11. Norway
12. Japan

UNITED STATES OLYMPIC STATS

Player	Goals	Assists	Points	Penalty
Mark Johnson	5	6	11	6
Buzzy Schneider	5	3	8	4
Rob McClanahan	5	3	8	2
Mark Pavelich	1	6	7	2
Dave Christian	0	7	7	6
John Harrington	0	6	6	2
Mike Eruzione	3	2	5	2
Phil Verchota	3	2	5	8
Dave Silk	2	3	5	0
Mark Wells	2	1	3	0
Neal Broten	2	1	3	2
Steve Christoff	2	1	3	6
Ken Morrow	1	2	3	6
Eric Strobel	1	2	3	2
Mike Ramsey	0	2	2	8
Bill Baker	1	0	1	4
Jack O'Callahan	0	1	1	2
Bob Suter	0	0	0	6
Jim Craig	0	0	0	2
USA	33	48	81	70
Opponents	15	19	34	64

Goaltending	GP	W	L	T	GA	Ave.	Saves	Ave.
Jim Craig	7	6	0	1	15	2.14	183	26
Opponents	7	0	6	1	33	4.71	194	28

POWER PLAY
By U.S.: 3 goals in 15 advantages (20%)
By Oppon.: 4 goals in 24 advantages (16.7%)

SCORING BY LINES	G	A	PTS
Schneider-Pavelich-Harrington	17	20	34
McClanahan-Johnson-Silk	14	14	28
Eruzione-Broten-Christoff	7	4	11
Verchota-Wells-Strobel	6	5	11

U. S. Shots	By U. S.	By Opponent
Vs. Sweden	29 (2)	36 (2)
Vs. Czechoslovakia	27 (7)	31 (3)
Vs. Norway	43 (5)	22 (1)
Vs. Romania	51 (7)	21 (2)
Vs. West Germany	32 (4)	26 (2)
Vs. Soviet Union	16 (4)	39 (3)
Vs. Finland	29 (4)	23 (2)

U.S. Shots			By U. S.				By Opponent	
By Period	*1*	*2*	*3*	*Tot*	*1*	*2*	*3*	*Tot*
Vs. Sweden	7	12	10	29	16	11	9	36
Vs. Czechoslovakia	11	5	11	27	13	6	12	31
Vs. Norway	16	16	11	43	9	7	6	22
Vs. Romania	20	16	15	51	9	9	3	21
Vs. West Germany	14	9	9	32	7	6	13	26
Vs. Soviet Union	8	2	6	16	18	12	9	39
Vs. Finland	14	8	7	29	7	6	10	23
TOTALS	90	68	69	227	79	57	62	198

U.S. Scoring			By U.S.				By Opponent	
By Period	*1*	*2*	*3*	*Tot*	*1*	*2*	*3*	*Tot*
Vs. Sweden	0	1	1	2	1	0	1	2
Vs. Czechoslovakia	2	2	3	7	2	0	1	3
Vs. Norway	0	3	2	5	1	0	0	1
Vs. Romania	2	2	3	7	0	1	1	2
Vs. West Germany	0	2	2	4	2	0	0	2
Vs. Soviet Union	2	0	2	4	2	1	0	3
Vs. Finland	0	1	3	4	1	1	0	2
Totals	6	11	16	33	9	3	3	15

—In six of the seven games, the U.S. gave up the first goal.

—Twenty-one of the 33 U.S. goals were scored in the first or last five minutes of a period, meaning 63.6% of the American scoring was done during the interval stressed by Coach Brooks.

—The clearest pattern of the Olympics was that of the U.S. team getting stronger over the last two periods. They outscored opponents 27-6 and outshot them 137-119.

—The Americans took 90 of their shots (39.6%) in the first period but scored only six times or 18.1% of their goals.

—Left wings produced 16 (or 48.5%) of the 33 U.S. goals; centers 10 (30.3%); right wings 5 (15.2%) and defensemen 2 (6%).

Acknowledgments

Thanks to Keith Bellows for giving me the assignment of a lifetime. Larry Hill and Mava Salmon made sure that this book first found a home, and Paul Dickson and John Grafton so delivered in that regard years later.

There's no better teacher of writing than Bill Glavin at Syracuse University, and no better friends in letters than Howard Mansfield, Bud Anzalone, Jim Naughton, Mark Derringer, Budd Bailey, Maura McEnaney, Sy Montgomery, Bob Reichblum and David Everett.

Thanks to Bob and Cindy Albiston, Chuck Bauerlein, Sara Elder, Gina Pera, Bonnie Holsinger, Brian Perry and Tina Poveromo for their support and friendship back in the day. Don Akchin and Pam Beaver took a chance on me early in my career, and I'm a better writer for their guidance and encouragement.

Finally, thanks to my parents and siblings, who taught me long ago to show up and always believe.

Books by Tim Wendel

FICTION

Red Rain
My Man Stan
Castro's Curveball

NONFICTION

Buffalo, Home of the Braves
Far From Home
The New Face of Baseball
Going for the Gold

About the Author

TIM WENDEL is the author of seven books, including the novels *Castro's Curveball* and *Red Rain*. His writing has appeared in *Esquire*, *The New York Times*, *GQ*, *Gargoyle* and *USA Today*, where he is on the op-ed page's board of contributors. A graduate of Johns Hopkins University, he teaches nonfiction and fiction writing there. Visit the author at www.timwendel.com.

A CATALOG OF SELECTED DOVER BOOKS IN ALL FIELDS OF INTEREST

CONCERNING THE SPIRITUAL IN ART, Wassily Kandinsky. Pioneering work by father of abstract art. Thoughts on color theory, nature of art. Analysis of earlier masters. 12 illustrations. 80pp. of text. 5⅜ x 8½. 0-486-23411-8

CELTIC ART: The Methods of Construction, George Bain. Simple geometric techniques for making Celtic interlacements, spirals, Kells-type initials, animals, humans, etc. Over 500 illustrations. 160pp. 9 x 12. (Available in U.S. only.) 0-486-22923-8

AN ATLAS OF ANATOMY FOR ARTISTS, Fritz Schider. Most thorough reference work on art anatomy in the world. Hundreds of illustrations, including selections from works by Vesalius, Leonardo, Goya, Ingres, Michelangelo, others. 593 illustrations. 192pp. 7⅛ x 10¼. 0-486-20241-0

CELTIC HAND STROKE-BY-STROKE (Irish Half-Uncial from "The Book of Kells"): An Arthur Baker Calligraphy Manual, Arthur Baker. Complete guide to creating each letter of the alphabet in distinctive Celtic manner. Covers hand position, strokes, pens, inks, paper, more. Illustrated. 48pp. 8¼ x 11. 0-486-24336-2

EASY ORIGAMI, John Montroll. Charming collection of 32 projects (hat, cup, pelican, piano, swan, many more) specially designed for the novice origami hobbyist. Clearly illustrated easy-to-follow instructions insure that even beginning papercrafters will achieve successful results. 48pp. 8¼ x 11. 0-486-27298-2

BLOOMINGDALE'S ILLUSTRATED 1886 CATALOG: Fashions, Dry Goods and Housewares, Bloomingdale Brothers. Famed merchants' extremely rare catalog depicting about 1,700 products: clothing, housewares, firearms, dry goods, jewelry, more. Invaluable for dating, identifying vintage items. Also, copyright-free graphics for artists, designers. Co-published with Henry Ford Museum & Greenfield Village. 160pp. 8¼ x 11. 0-486-25780-0

THE ART OF WORLDLY WISDOM, Baltasar Gracian. "Think with the few and speak with the many," "Friends are a second existence," and "Be able to forget" are among this 1637 volume's 300 pithy maxims. A perfect source of mental and spiritual refreshment, it can be opened at random and appreciated either in brief or at length. 128pp. 5⅜ x 8½. 0-486-44034-6

JOHNSON'S DICTIONARY: A Modern Selection, Samuel Johnson (E. L. McAdam and George Milne, eds.). This modern version reduces the original 1755 edition's 2,300 pages of definitions and literary examples to a more manageable length, retaining the verbal pleasure and historical curiosity of the original. 480pp. 5³⁄₁₆ x 8¼. 0-486-44089-3

ADVENTURES OF HUCKLEBERRY FINN, Mark Twain, Illustrated by E. W. Kemble. A work of eternal richness and complexity, a source of ongoing critical debate, and a literary landmark, Twain's 1885 masterpiece about a barefoot boy's journey of self-discovery has enthralled readers around the world. This handsome clothbound reproduction of the first edition features all 174 of the original black-and-white illustrations. 368pp. 5⅜ x 8½. 0-486-44322-1

CATALOG OF DOVER BOOKS

STICKLEY CRAFTSMAN FURNITURE CATALOGS, Gustav Stickley and L. & J. G. Stickley. Beautiful, functional furniture in two authentic catalogs from 1910. 594 illustrations, including 277 photos, show settles, rockers, armchairs, reclining chairs, bookcases, desks, tables. 183pp. 6½ x 9¼. 0-486-23838-5

AMERICAN LOCOMOTIVES IN HISTORIC PHOTOGRAPHS: 1858 to 1949, Ron Ziel (ed.). A rare collection of 126 meticulously detailed official photographs, called "builder portraits," of American locomotives that majestically chronicle the rise of steam locomotive power in America. Introduction. Detailed captions. xi+ 129pp. 9 x 12. 0-486-27393-8

AMERICA'S LIGHTHOUSES: An Illustrated History, Francis Ross Holland, Jr. Delightfully written, profusely illustrated fact-filled survey of over 200 American lighthouses since 1716. History, anecdotes, technological advances, more. 240pp. 8 x 10¾. 0-486-25576-X

TOWARDS A NEW ARCHITECTURE, Le Corbusier. Pioneering manifesto by founder of "International School." Technical and aesthetic theories, views of industry, economics, relation of form to function, "mass-production split" and much more. Profusely illustrated. 320pp. 6⅛ x 9¼. (Available in U.S. only.) 0-486-25023-7

HOW THE OTHER HALF LIVES, Jacob Riis. Famous journalistic record, exposing poverty and degradation of New York slums around 1900, by major social reformer. 100 striking and influential photographs. 233pp. 10 x 7⅞. 0-486-22012-5

FRUIT KEY AND TWIG KEY TO TREES AND SHRUBS, William M. Harlow. One of the handiest and most widely used identification aids. Fruit key covers 120 deciduous and evergreen species; twig key 160 deciduous species. Easily used. Over 300 photographs. 126pp. 5⅜ x 8½. 0-486-20511-8

COMMON BIRD SONGS, Dr. Donald J. Borror. Songs of 60 most common U.S. birds: robins, sparrows, cardinals, bluejays, finches, more—arranged in order of increasing complexity. Up to 9 variations of songs of each species.
Cassette and manual 0-486-99911-4

ORCHIDS AS HOUSE PLANTS, Rebecca Tyson Northen. Grow cattleyas and many other kinds of orchids—in a window, in a case, or under artificial light. 63 illustrations. 148pp. 5⅜ x 8½. 0-486-23261-1

MONSTER MAZES, Dave Phillips. Masterful mazes at four levels of difficulty. Avoid deadly perils and evil creatures to find magical treasures. Solutions for all 32 exciting illustrated puzzles. 48pp. 8¼ x 11. 0-486-26005-4

MOZART'S DON GIOVANNI (DOVER OPERA LIBRETTO SERIES), Wolfgang Amadeus Mozart. Introduced and translated by Ellen H. Bleiler. Standard Italian libretto, with complete English translation. Convenient and thoroughly portable—an ideal companion for reading along with a recording or the performance itself. Introduction. List of characters. Plot summary. 121pp. 5¼ x 8½. 0-486-24944-1

FRANK LLOYD WRIGHT'S DANA HOUSE, Donald Hoffmann. Pictorial essay of residential masterpiece with over 160 interior and exterior photos, plans, elevations, sketches and studies. 128pp. 9¼ x 10¾. 0-486-29120-0

THE CLARINET AND CLARINET PLAYING, David Pino. Lively, comprehensive work features suggestions about technique, musicianship, and musical interpretation, as well as guidelines for teaching, making your own reeds, and preparing for public performance. Includes an intriguing look at clarinet history. "A godsend," *The Clarinet,* Journal of the International Clarinet Society. Appendixes. 7 illus. 320pp. 5⅜ x 8½. 0-486-40270-3

HOLLYWOOD GLAMOR PORTRAITS, John Kobal (ed.). 145 photos from 1926-49. Harlow, Gable, Bogart, Bacall; 94 stars in all. Full background on photographers, technical aspects. 160pp. 8⅜ x 11¼. 0-486-23352-9

THE RAVEN AND OTHER FAVORITE POEMS, Edgar Allan Poe. Over 40 of the author's most memorable poems: "The Bells," "Ulalume," "Israfel," "To Helen," "The Conqueror Worm," "Eldorado," "Annabel Lee," many more. Alphabetic lists of titles and first lines. 64pp. 5³⁄₁₆ x 8¼. 0-486-26685-0

PERSONAL MEMOIRS OF U. S. GRANT, Ulysses Simpson Grant. Intelligent, deeply moving firsthand account of Civil War campaigns, considered by many the finest military memoirs ever written. Includes letters, historic photographs, maps and more. 528pp. 6⅛ x 9¼. 0-486-28587-1

POE ILLUSTRATED: Art by Doré, Dulac, Rackham and Others, selected and edited by Jeff A. Menges. More than 100 compelling illustrations, in brilliant color and crisp black-and-white, include scenes from "The Raven," "The Pit and the Pendulum," "The Gold-Bug," and other stories and poems. 96pp. 8⅜ x 11.
0-486-45746-X

RUSSIAN STORIES/RUSSKIE RASSKAZY: A Dual-Language Book, edited by Gleb Struve. Twelve tales by such masters as Chekhov, Tolstoy, Dostoevsky, Pushkin, others. Excellent word-for-word English translations on facing pages, plus teaching and study aids, Russian/English vocabulary, biographical/critical introductions, more. 416pp. 5⅜ x 8½. 0-486-26244-8

PHILADELPHIA THEN AND NOW: 60 Sites Photographed in the Past and Present, Kenneth Finkel and Susan Oyama. Rare photographs of City Hall, Logan Square, Independence Hall, Betsy Ross House, other landmarks juxtaposed with contemporary views. Captures changing face of historic city. Introduction. Captions. 128pp. 8¼ x 11. 0-486-25790-8

NORTH AMERICAN INDIAN LIFE: Customs and Traditions of 23 Tribes, Elsie Clews Parsons (ed.). 27 fictionalized essays by noted anthropologists examine religion, customs, government, additional facets of life among the Winnebago, Crow, Zuni, Eskimo, other tribes. 480pp. 6⅛ x 9¼. 0-486-27377-6

TECHNICAL MANUAL AND DICTIONARY OF CLASSICAL BALLET, Gail Grant. Defines, explains, comments on steps, movements, poses and concepts. 15-page pictorial section. Basic book for student, viewer. 127pp. 5⅜ x 8½.
0-486-21843-0

THE MALE AND FEMALE FIGURE IN MOTION: 60 Classic Photographic Sequences, Eadweard Muybridge. 60 true-action photographs of men and women walking, running, climbing, bending, turning, etc., reproduced from a rare 19th-century masterpiece. vi + 121pp. 9 x 12. 0-486-24745-7

CATALOG OF DOVER BOOKS

ANIMALS: 1,419 Copyright-Free Illustrations of Mammals, Birds, Fish, Insects, etc., Jim Harter (ed.). Clear wood engravings present, in extremely lifelike poses, over 1,000 species of animals. One of the most extensive pictorial sourcebooks of its kind. Captions. Index. 284pp. 9 x 12. 0-486-23766-4

1001 QUESTIONS ANSWERED ABOUT THE SEASHORE, N. J. Berrill and Jacquelyn Berrill. Queries answered about dolphins, sea snails, sponges, starfish, fishes, shore birds, many others. Covers appearance, breeding, growth, feeding, much more. 305pp. 5¼ x 8¼. 0-486-23366-9

ATTRACTING BIRDS TO YOUR YARD, William J. Weber. Easy-to-follow guide offers advice on how to attract the greatest diversity of birds: birdhouses, feeders, water and waterers, much more. 96pp. 5³⁄₁₆ x 8¼. 0-486-28927-3

MEDICINAL AND OTHER USES OF NORTH AMERICAN PLANTS: A Historical Survey with Special Reference to the Eastern Indian Tribes, Charlotte Erichsen-Brown. Chronological historical citations document 500 years of usage of plants, trees, shrubs native to eastern Canada, northeastern U.S. Also complete identifying information. 343 illustrations. 544pp. 6½ x 9¼. 0-486-25951-X

STORYBOOK MAZES, Dave Phillips. 23 stories and mazes on two-page spreads: Wizard of Oz, Treasure Island, Robin Hood, etc. Solutions. 64pp. 8¼ x 11. 0-486-23628-5

AMERICAN NEGRO SONGS: 230 Folk Songs and Spirituals, Religious and Secular, John W. Work. This authoritative study traces the African influences of songs sung and played by black Americans at work, in church, and as entertainment. The author discusses the lyric significance of such songs as "Swing Low, Sweet Chariot," "John Henry," and others and offers the words and music for 230 songs. Bibliography. Index of Song Titles. 272pp. 6½ x 9¼. 0-486-40271-1

MOVIE-STAR PORTRAITS OF THE FORTIES, John Kobal (ed.). 163 glamor, studio photos of 106 stars of the 1940s: Rita Hayworth, Ava Gardner, Marlon Brando, Clark Gable, many more. 176pp. 8⅜ x 11¼. 0-486-23546-7

YEKL and THE IMPORTED BRIDEGROOM AND OTHER STORIES OF YIDDISH NEW YORK, Abraham Cahan. Film Hester Street based on Yekl (1896). Novel, other stories among first about Jewish immigrants on N.Y.'s East Side. 240pp. 5⅜ x 8½. 0-486-22427-9

SELECTED POEMS, Walt Whitman. Generous sampling from Leaves of Grass. Twenty-four poems include "I Hear America Singing," "Song of the Open Road," "I Sing the Body Electric," "When Lilacs Last in the Dooryard Bloom'd," "O Captain! My Captain!"—all reprinted from an authoritative edition. Lists of titles and first lines. 128pp. 5³⁄₁₆ x 8¼. 0-486-26878-0

SONGS OF EXPERIENCE: Facsimile Reproduction with 26 Plates in Full Color, William Blake. 26 full-color plates from a rare 1826 edition. Includes "The Tyger," "London," "Holy Thursday," and other poems. Printed text of poems. 48pp. 5¼ x 7. 0-486-24636-1

THE BEST TALES OF HOFFMANN, E. T. A. Hoffmann. 10 of Hoffmann's most important stories: "Nutcracker and the King of Mice," "The Golden Flowerpot," etc. 458pp. 5⅜ x 8½. 0-486-21793-0

THE BOOK OF TEA, Kakuzo Okakura. Minor classic of the Orient: entertaining, charming explanation, interpretation of traditional Japanese culture in terms of tea ceremony. 94pp. 5⅜ x 8½. 0-486-20070-1

HOW TO DO BEADWORK, Mary White. Fundamental book on craft from simple projects to five-bead chains and woven works. 106 illustrations. 142pp. 5⅜ x 8.
0-486-20697-1

THE 1912 AND 1915 GUSTAV STICKLEY FURNITURE CATALOGS, Gustav Stickley. With over 200 detailed illustrations and descriptions, these two catalogs are essential reading and reference materials and identification guides for Stickley furniture. Captions cite materials, dimensions and prices. 112pp. 6½ x 9¼. 0-486-26676-1

SIX GREAT DIALOGUES: Apology, Crito, Phaedo, Phaedrus, Symposium, The Republic, Plato, translated by Benjamin Jowett. Plato's Dialogues rank among Western civilization's most important and influential philosophical works. These 6 selections of his major works explore a broad range of enduringly relevant issues. Authoritative Jowett translations. 480pp. 5³⁄₁₆ x 8¼. 0-486-45465-7

DEMONOLATRY: An Account of the Historical Practice of Witchcraft, Nicolas Remy, edited with an Introduction and Notes by Montague Summers, translated by E. A. Ashwin. This extremely influential 1595 study was frequently cited at witchcraft trials. In addition to lurid details of satanic pacts and sexual perversity, it presents the particulars of numerous court cases. 240pp. 6½ x 9¼. 0-486-46137-8

VICTORIAN FASHIONS AND COSTUMES FROM HARPER'S BAZAAR, 1867–1898, Stella Blum (ed.). Day costumes, evening wear, sports clothes, shoes, hats, other accessories in over 1,000 detailed engravings. 320pp. 9⅜ x 12¼.
0-486-22990-4

THE LONG ISLAND RAIL ROAD IN EARLY PHOTOGRAPHS, Ron Ziel. Over 220 rare photos, informative text document origin (1844) and development of rail service on Long Island. Vintage views of early trains, locomotives, stations, passengers, crews, much more. Captions. 8⅞ x 11¾. 0-486-26301-0

VOYAGE OF THE LIBERDADE, Joshua Slocum. Great 19th-century mariner's thrilling, first-hand account of the wreck of his ship off South America, the 35-foot boat he built from the wreckage, and its remarkable voyage home. 128pp. 5⅜ x 8½.
0-486-40022-0

TEN BOOKS ON ARCHITECTURE, Vitruvius. The most important book ever written on architecture. Early Roman aesthetics, technology, classical orders, site selection, all other aspects. Morgan translation. 331pp. 5⅜ x 8½. 0-486-20645-9

THE HUMAN FIGURE IN MOTION, Eadweard Muybridge. More than 4,500 stopped-action photos, in action series, showing undraped men, women, children jumping, lying down, throwing, sitting, wrestling, carrying, etc. 390pp. 7⅞ x 10⅝.
0-486-20204-6 Clothbd.

TREES OF THE EASTERN AND CENTRAL UNITED STATES AND CANADA, William M. Harlow. Best one-volume guide to 140 trees. Full descriptions, woodlore, range, etc. Over 600 illustrations. Handy size. 288pp. 4½ x 6⅜. 0-486-20395-6

MY FIRST BOOK OF TCHAIKOVSKY: Favorite Pieces in Easy Piano Arrangements, edited by David Dutkanicz. These special arrangements of favorite Tchaikovsky themes are ideal for beginner pianists, child or adult. Contents include themes from "The Nutcracker," "March Slav," Symphonies Nos. 5 and 6, "Swan Lake," "Sleeping Beauty," and more. 48pp. 8¼ x 11. 0-486-46416-4

BIG BOOK OF MAZES AND LABYRINTHS, Walter Shepherd. 50 mazes and labyrinths in all–classical, solid, ripple, and more–in one great volume. Perfect inexpensive puzzler for clever youngsters. Full solutions. 112pp. 8⅛ x 11. 0-486-22951-3

PIANO TUNING, J. Cree Fischer. Clearest, best book for beginner, amateur. Simple repairs, raising dropped notes, tuning by easy method of flattened fifths. No previous skills needed. 4 illustrations. 201pp. 5⅜ x 8½. 0-486-23267-0